2022 Writing Contest

A Diversity of Expression

Stories and Poetry from across the U.S.

SouthWest Writers
Carlisle Executive Offices
3200 Carlisle Blvd N.E.
Albuquerque, New Mexico 87110
www.southwestwriters.com

A Diversity of Expression
Rose Marie Kern, Contest Chairwoman
RMK Publications, Editing & Formatting
ISBN: 9798841432357

The 2022 Writing Contest

The motto of SouthWest Writers is "Writers Helping Writers." We do this through classes, conferences, workshops and a membership of more than 430 people—many of whom are published, well-known authors. Twice monthly meetings offer insights and opportunities for networking.

The Annual Writing Contest offers an important step in an author's development. It focuses on short pieces of poetry, non-fiction essays and genre-driven short prose. The contest allows both budding authors and seasoned writers to sharpen their skills.

Thirteen categories were adjudicated, and awards were given for First, Second and Third place and Honorable Mention.

Many new authors need a challenge in a supportive environment where they can feel comfortable discussing their work. A true success story begins with being courageous enough to put your skills in front of others. Our words are our children, so we need to understand that constructive criticism does not condemn, it helps us mold and grow out talents.

Seasoned published writers can fall into a rut. Contests such as this one channel their minds and talents in different directions, freshening their skills and pushing their boundaries. Our contests are open to anyone, not just members of SWW.

This year in addition to prose, poetry and non-fiction, SWW included two art categories. Most of the categories were reviewed by our professional team but three categories were adjudicated by the membership at large.

These stories and poems are fun, or sad, or factual, or surprising, many of them are all these things. Pay attention to the names of the authors, you will probably see them again!

Acknowledgements

SouthWest Writers is fortunate to have members who are not only published authors but also editors, photographers, proofreaders and formatters. The following members contributed these skills to the production of the 2019 SWW *Winners Anthology.*

Writing contest organizing committee:
Rose Marie Kern, Chair
Brenda Cole
Kathy Shuit
Cornelia Gamlem
Patricia Walkow

Office Support: ReVaH Loring

To learn more about what SouthWest Writers has to offer go to:

www.southwestwriters.com

Table of Contents

Section Thirteen Non-Fiction Memoir 246

ARTWORK

Part of this year's contest included a opportunity for people to send images which were to be included in this book. The SouthWest Writers Membership voted for their top five – which you will see scattered about the book.

The photographer/artists who submitted them received payment for their use. Below is a listing of the images - their artist/photographers and the page number on which you can view them. Other images were added by the Contest Committee as needed.

Page	Image	Submitted By
78	Hamblett Cabin, Aztec, NM	Rebecca Larivee
144	Flyers	Jeffry Otis
188	Sandia Mountains	Jette Tritten
206	Looking for Company	Robert Cudney
226	Wildly Shining	Elizabeth S. Layton

Judging

Part of SWW's mandate of "Writers Helping Writers" is to prepare new authors for what to expect when they submit their work to magazines or book publishers. We encourage all writers to begin their journey with an understanding of what will be expected of a professional. To that end, our contest closely follows the process of many publishers.

All contest entries are reviewed first by a "gatekeeper" who ensures the submission satisfies Contest and Category Rules concerning type style and size, line spacing, word count requirements and what is allowed on the page. If the entry did not meet those rules, it would not be sent on for subsequent judging. Entries that do not meet requirements are disqualified.

After the initial round of judging, the top scoring pieces are set aside to be considered by the contest committee. These finalists were announced in the *SouthWest Sage* newsletter and on the SWW website. All finalists had the option of having their work included in this anthology. The number of winners in each category is determined by the Writing Contest Committee according to established criteria

Our judges look for writing that emphasizes creative and intelligent use of the English language to create mood and craft an effective story line. They were encouraged to provide critiques which are available to contestants after the awards ceremony.

The Writing Contest Team

You can tell a lot about a writing contest by the quality of its judges. SouthWest Writers is honored to have a team of award-winning published authors and professional editors that cross all genres. We want to thank them for the hours they spent judging the entries and leaving constructive criticism for all participants.

*****

Chris Allen, a retired archaeologist, started writing short stories in 2014. Since then, she has won awards for both storytelling and editing. Her latest book, Alchemy's Reach, will be published in 2023 in paperback, e-book, and as an audiobook. She resides in Corrales, New Mexico, with her husband and a menagerie of sheep, goats, horses, and dogs.

~~~~~

Parris Afton Bonds is the mother of five sons and the author of more than fifty published novels. She is co-founder and first vice president of **Romance Writers of America,** as well as, co-founder of **Southwest Writers**. Her latest publication is *The Banshees*, Vol. V of *The Texicans* saga.

~~~~~

Joe Brown writes historical fiction and memoirs. He's retired from his USAF military and civil service careers in 2010 as a Senior Analyst advising the Commander, USAF Flight Test Center. He's a member of SouthWest Writers, Western Writers of America, Military Writers Society of America, and several other non-profit organizations.

~~~~~

With fifteen years of editorial expertise, **Brenda Cole** began her writing career at The University of Wisconsin. The majority of her work is in Life Sciences and non-fiction. During lockdown she discovered a flair for flash fiction. She has won numerous awards and accolades and is currently President of SouthWest Writers.

Anna DiBella, NLAPW national president 2004-2006, has been involved in advocacy in the arts for the past 50 years. An author of four volumes of poetry, she edits, lectures, and presents poetry workshops nationally. She has also curated numerous art exhibitions and has served as judge for both art and poetry.

~~~~~

Management consultant and speaker, **Cornelia Gamlem**, took her expertise and shared it through her award-winning books. She coauthored three editions of her first book plus four more. Three have been translated into other languages. Two were recognized by the internationally acclaimed The Next Generation Indie Book Awards. www.bigbookofhr.com

~~~~~

An advocate for those with invisible illnesses, **Dr. Thelma Giomi**, is involved in Patients' Rights, Lupus Research, and is a founding member of Cancer Support Now. Her work offers pathways to resilience and hope through both her award-winning novels and collections of poetry. For information on her books go to www.thelmagiomi.com

~~~~~

In addition to authoring several books and over a thousand published articles, **Rose Marie Kern** owns **RMK Publications.** On the board of SouthWest Writers for over a decade, she is their current writing contest chairperson. Rose has won many local and national writing competitions. www.rmkpublications.com

~~~~~

Former newspaper reporter and editor, **Christina Laurie**, publishes haiku, receiving many prizes and accolades. Her poetry book, *Purr Poems: Kittens and Cats* features poems and haiku. She authored two children's books: *C is for Cape Cod* and *The Lobsters' Night Before Christmas.* Her current project is a children's book about *Lucertia Coffin Mott: The First Suffragette.*

~~~~~

Elizabeth S. Layton is a published poet and the author of several short stories. She received her Bachelor of Arts in Mass Communication with a minor in Science from Fort Lewis College and her Masters in Creative Writing in Film, Television, and Gaming from Full Sail University. You can visit her online at www.elizabethlaytonwriter.com.

In addition to writing them, **Jaqueline Murray Loring** reviews screenplays and poetry. She serves as a SouthWest Writers board member and she was the 2020 recipient of the Parris Award, SouthWest Writers' most prestigious honor. Her book *Vietnam Veterans Unbroken: Conversations on Trauma and Resiliency* won the 2021 NM-AZ Book Award for Current Events/Politics.

RJ Mirabal has been a member of Southwest Writers and SCBWI for several years. His New Mexico-based *Rio Grande Parallax* adult fantasy series as well as young reader books—***Trixie Finds Her People, Trixie: Round Brown Ball of Dog,*** and ***Dragon Train*** — were finalists in NM/AZ and NMPW contests.

Carol Holland March authors fantasy novels, short stories, and personal essays. This year her book, ***When Spirit Whispers***, was released as part of her *Healing from Trauma* series. Her short story, ***Sisters***, will soon appear in *New Myths* online magazine. Carol teaches creativity, storytelling, and memoir at UNM Continuing Education. She is a book coach and editor.

Sam Moorman has a Journalism B.A. and Creative Writing M.A. from San Francisco State University. but chose construction as a career. He returned to writing in retirement and publishes poems and stories in various outlets.

Award-winning editor, **Benjamin Radford** is also the author or co-author of thirteen books, most recently ***America the Fearful: Media and the Marketing of National Panics***. He holds Masters degrees in education and public health, and is co-host of *Squaring the Strange* podcast.

Author, editor, and artist **Kathy Louise Schuit** says one key to quickly discovering the difference between mundane and great writing is finding beta readers who will tell you the unvarnished truth. The results are evident in her editing of SWW's award winning newsletter, *The Sage*, combined with her beautifully written and designed children's books.   ~~~~~

Rob Spiegel is a full time writer living in Albuquerque. He works as senior editor for *Design News.* His fiction, poetry, memoir, and drama have been published in such diverse publications as *Gargoyle, Fleas on the Dog, Rolling Stone*, and *True Confessions.*

Lynne Sturtevant is the author of five nonfiction books and two contemporary fantasy novels. Before moving to New Mexico, she owned a travel agency, a consulting service for local historians, and a ghost tour company. In addition to writing, she designs websites for creative people over 50.

Patricia Walkow is an award-winning author of newspaper and magazine articles, short stories, and full-length works of fiction and narrative non-fiction. She is both editor and contributor to many anthologies, some of which have won awards. She has two new novels in progress, as well as an anthology of short stories. Ms. Walkow's next scheduled publication is a mystery/romance she co-authored. It will be published by Austin Macauley in 2023.

Dan Wetmore has been a judge for SWW's contest four years running, was on the committee for three, and chair in 2021. He hosts the Wordwrights critique group and has authored two poetry volumes: "My Mother's Gentle Unbecoming" (tied for 1st in the New Mexico-Arizona Book Awards), and "Phoboudenopanophobia". https://www.southwestwriters.com/author-pages-n-z/dan-wetmore

Dollie Williams currently works as a support specialist for a local software company. She has published 2 novels in the science fiction Chesan Legacy Series: ***Child of Chaos***, which won the New Mexico Arizona Book Award for Best Science Fiction in 2015, and ***Chaos Unleashed***. She is currently working on book 3, ***Chosen Son***.

A Diversity of Expression

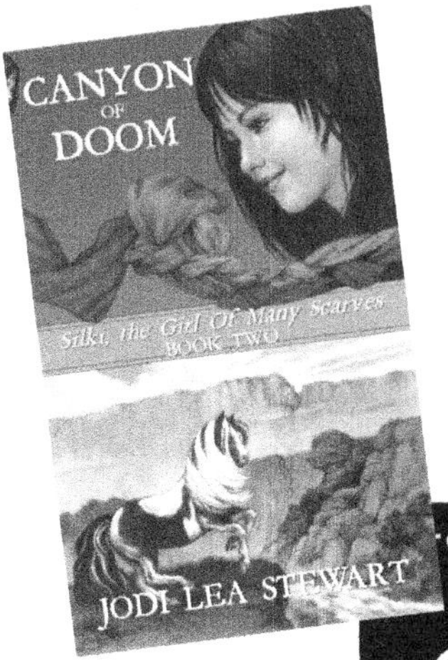
CANYON
OF
DOOM
Silki, the Girl Of Many Scarves
BOOK TWO
JODI LEA STEWART

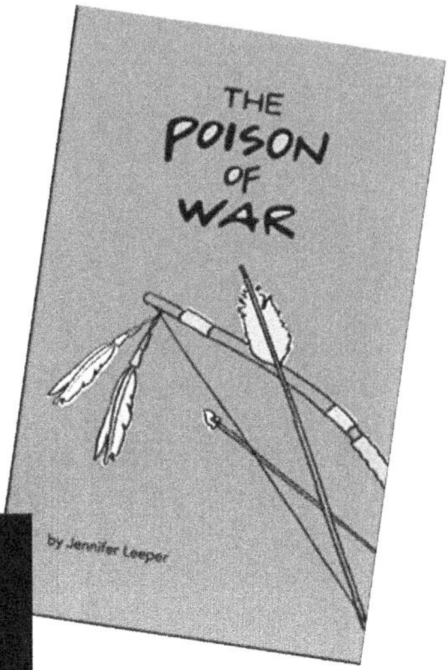
THE
POISON
OF
WAR
by Jennifer Leeper

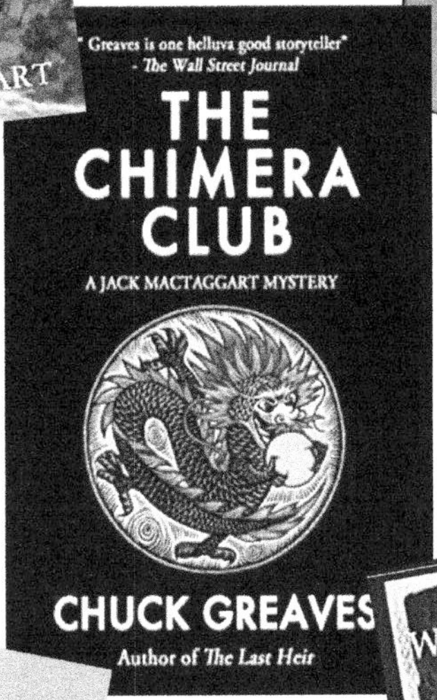
" Greaves is one helluva good storyteller"
- The Wall Street Journal
THE
CHIMERA
CLUB
A JACK MACTAGGART MYSTERY
CHUCK GREAVES
Author of The Last Heir

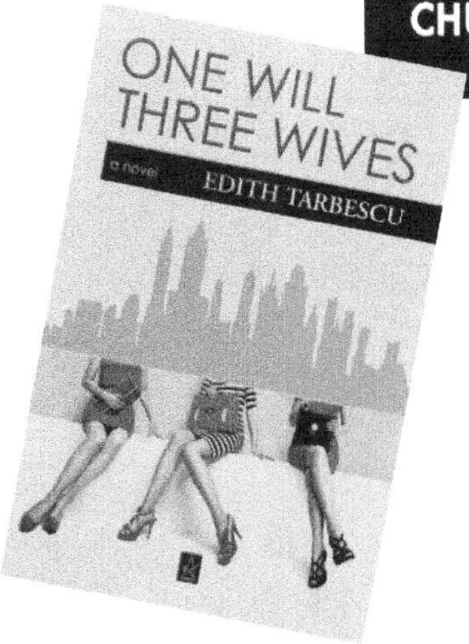
ONE WILL
THREE WIVES
a novel
EDITH TARBESCU

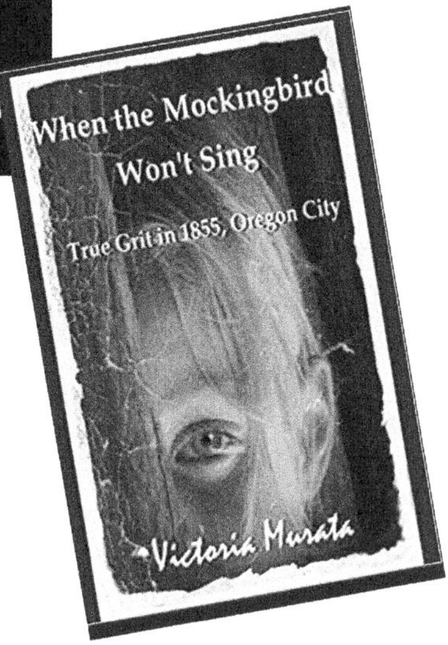
When the Mockingbird
Won't Sing
True Grit in 1855, Oregon City
Victoria Murata

Section One

Opening Chapter of a Previously Published Book

This year SouthWest Writers gave authors the chance to submit the opening chapter of a book they had published between 2019 and 2022. In a sense all of them were winners because they had written a book and already negotiated the pathways to publication.

Some of these winners were self-published, and some were accepted by traditional publishers. If you enjoy these first chapters, the information where you can find the rest of the book is located along with the author bio at the end.

1ˢᵗ Place Winner   **Chuck Greaves**

The Chimera Club

After Bernadette had announced in an urgent whisper that a Mae Gallagher was here to see me but before I could remind her that this wasn't Supercuts and that we don't accept walk-ins off the street, Mayday leaned into the intercom on my desk and instructed, "Send her in."

"The Ari Goldstone murder," she said, moving from the client chair opposite my desk to the sofa against the wall. "Hello? Daughter of Jimmy Kwan."

That I hadn't recognized the Gallagher name was not surprising since it evoked, at least in my imagination, a mental image of ginger hair and freckles. There also was the fact that I'd been in trial up in Sacramento for the past three weeks while the media frenzy surrounding the Goldstone murder was consuming L.A. like Godzilla. The latest remake of which, come to think of it, might have been an Ari Goldstone production, but before I could put that question to Mayday, Bernie knocked and swung the door open and stepped aside with a sweep of her arm as though she were ushering royalty.

Jimmy Kwan's daughter was younger than I'd expected – maybe late twenties at most. Tall and willowy, she strode the carpeted distance from the doorway to my desk with the ramrod posture and swinging hips of the runway model she'd been. Her raven hair was long and sleek and parted on the side, leaving but one Eurasian eye with which to navigate.

My first impression was of a woman used to being stared at, and that this morning would be no exception.

"Mr. MacTaggart. Thank you for seeing me without an appointment."

"Jack, please. And the pleasure's mine." I nodded to Mayday as I stood. "My partner, Marta Suarez."

She shook our hands in turn and took the chair Mayday had vacated, plunking a pricey-looking handbag in her lap. She tossed her hair and crossed her exquisite legs. She wore no jewelry that I could see, and her navy skirt and starched linen blouse were stylish yet conservative, the overall effect being that of long-stemmed roses wrapped in newsprint.

Or maybe it was nuclear fission encased in lead, for public safety.

"I'll come straight to the point," she said in a velvety voice inflected with a faintly British accent. "My father, as you probably know, has been arrested for Ari Goldstone's murder. He didn't do it, and he can prove he didn't do it, so there's no reason he should be sitting in jail right now like, like . . ."

"Like a man who's guilty of murder?" I suggested, bailing her out.

"Exactly. Which of course he isn't."

"Why is he still in custody?" I'd addressed that one to Mayday, who was working the iPad tablet in her lap like a concert pianist. "He should've made bail days ago."

Mayday turned the screen to face me. "According to the news reports, Mr. Kwan hasn't sought bail and is fully cooperating with the authorities. He's apparently refused all visitors, including family. Rumor has it that a plea deal is imminent."

"It's true that he won't see me," our visitor said, "but the rest can't possibly be right. I told you he's innocent. You can't plead guilty to a crime you didn't commit, can you?"

You could, of course, but I rarely recommended it to my own clients. From what little I knew of the Goldstone case, the infamous Jimmy Kwan had been arrested five days earlier upon his return from Hong Kong where, according to multiple business associates, he'd been visiting for over a week. Meaning he'd been seven thousand miles from the Hotel Bel-Air in Los Angeles when the producer's naked body was discovered by a hotel maid, its wrists and ankles bound to the bedposts and twelve stab wounds dimpling its fat and hairy abdomen.

"Any idea why they arrested your father in the first place? I mean, had he and Goldstone ever done business together? Did they even know each other?"

"No," she said, "and that's what's been so frustrating. I've tried calling the District Attorney's office, but nobody there will talk to me. I went to the jail, but they turned me away. Even the woman who questioned me isn't returning my calls."

"The woman who questioned you?"

"A police detective." She opened her bag and fished a business card from inside. "A very nice black woman. Shonda Robbins."

"When was that?"

"Last Monday. Two days before my father's arrest. She asked after my whereabouts on the night Ari was murdered, but mostly she wanted to know about Father. Where he was, whether he knew Ari – that sort of thing. I thought that was strange. I explained to her that I hadn't spoken to my father in years."

"Okay," I said, coming straight to a point of my own. "So what is it you'd like us to do?"

The question seemed to surprise her. "I want you to represent him, of course. There's obviously been a mistake. He has an alibi. I want you to get him out of jail, and then I want you to do whatever it takes to defend him."

She returned to her bag and removed two letter-sized envelopes, handing one across the desk. I sat back and extracted the cashier's check from inside. Ten thousand dollars, payable to MacTaggart & Suarez, LLP.

I was liking her more by the minute.

"I've asked around, Mr. MacTaggart, and you have quite the reputation. I've also heard that you and the District Attorney are friends. I know that confirming my father's alibi will involve some expense. I hope that's enough to get started."

I returned the check to its envelope and set both on the desk between us.

"Call me Jack. And yes, that's enough to get started. But your father doesn't appear to want visitors, let alone an attorney. If he won't see his own daughter, what makes you think he'll see me?"

By way of an answer she laid the second envelope next to the first one and pushed it toward me with a lacquered fingernail.

"Give him this. If you do, I think he'll at least talk to you."

Scrawled on the front of the second envelope was the word *Father* in a distinctive, slanting script.

"You need to understand something," I told her. "Even if I could find a way to get this to your father, the authorities will open it first."

"That's all right," she said. "You can open it now if you'd like."

I tapped the envelope against my blotter. As an old mentor once warned me, the law would be a splendid profession if not for the unhappy necessity of having clients. Meaning that even under the best of circumstances, clients can be demanding, impatient, ungrateful, and general pains in the ass, with criminal clients the worst of the lot. Jimmy Kwan, the so-called Chinese Bernie Madoff, was a convicted felon and a certified lowlife and now, very possibly, a brutal knife murderer. Worse, he was holed up in a cell downtown refusing to talk to anyone but the cops and the prosecutors, which made him either stupid or suicidal, and very possibly both.

Did I really need a guy like that in my life right now?

On the other side of the ledger, the Ari Goldstone murder was the hottest ticket in town, and whatever it was that District Attorney Gabriel Montoya had on Kwan, it must've been pretty compelling to warrant an arrest in the face of what seemed like an ironclad alibi. That made the case interesting. What made the case fascinating was the beautiful young woman sitting across the desk from me with the anxious look in her eye. So maybe I did need Jimmy Kwan in my life right now. I mean, how bad could the guy really be?

"Two more things you need to understand," I told her, again sinking back in my chair. "If I agree to take your father's case, then it's your father who'll be my client, not you, and therein lies an important distinction. For example, whatever's said between you and me isn't subject to the attorney-client privilege. That means if you're ever questioned under oath about any of our conversations, including this one, you'll have to answer fully and truthfully."

"All right. I think I understand."

"Did you ever play a game called Telephone when you were a girl? It's where you sit in a circle of friends and whisper a secret, and by the time it comes all the way back to you, it's a totally different message?"

"I suppose I did."

"Good. Point number two is that you're not to discuss our conversations with anyone, even with people you trust, because they too would have to answer truthfully if questioned and God only knows what they'd say. The same goes for phone calls, emails, or text messages. In other words, don't discuss your father's case with anyone, and from now on that includes the police. If they contact you again, just refer them to me and I'll make some arrangements on your behalf."

She nodded. "All right, I get the picture."

I studied her for a moment longer, then took up my letter opener and slipped it under the flap. Inside the second envelope was a folded sheet of cream-colored stationery with the words *Jack MacTaggart* scrawled in that same distinctive script. That was it – the entire message – except for the three printed words centered in shiny green ink at the top of the page:

*****

Author

Chuck Greaves won the grand-prize Storyteller Award in SWW's 2010 Writing Contest with his debut novel HUSH MONEY, later acquired by St. Martin's Minotaur. Six novels later, Chuck has been a finalist for most of the major awards in crime fiction including the Lefty, Shamus, Audie, and Macavity, as well as the Harper Lee Prize for legal fiction.

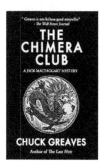

The Chimera Club was published in 2022 – it is the fourth installment of Chuck Greaves Jack MacTaggart series of legal mysteries. It is available at local bookstores, Amazon, and Barnes&Noble.com. To learn more, please visit Chuck at www.chuckgreaves.com

2nd Place Winner   **Jennifer Leeper**

The Poison of War

The two bodies lay in plain sight of the shuttered Salt Bingo Casino, though there were no witnesses other than a coyote and its jackrabbit prey. The two bodies lay still until the sun cracked its light over the Arizona desert like a great sky egg.

A pair of hikers discovered Joaquin Carrillo and Diego Velazquez weighted with eight pounds of Mexican-grown heroin on a Sunday morning. They lay in the upper Sonora on the periphery of the Tohono O'odham Indian Reservation. A single arrow pierced a vital organ inside each of the deceased.

Detective Frank Silva examined the entry site of an arrow lodged in Joaquin's left gut, eyeing a matching arrow in Diego's side. Frank rose slowly on aging knees. A gray and black braid snaked down the back of his denim shirt.

"Not even a footprint," Frank muttered to himself. "And they left the wallets and heroin, so it wasn't a payday. Could be a message to someone."

"The high school kids are making bows the old way now." Detective Arturo Vega nodded toward the bodies. He stood several inches shorter than his older partner, his black hair shaved close to his head. The men shared the wide, sweeping features of *Papago-Pima* ancestry.

"I thought they shot with compounds," said Frank moving out of the way of the body as a crime scene technician began dusting for prints. His feet kicked up dust as he looked for indications of a struggle such as smashed vegetation or blood. There wasn't so much as a bent prickly pear pad, though, and the only red came from the natural stain of desert ground around the crime scene.

"For their college archery scholarship money, but they shoot the old way when they're chasing down rabbits," said Arturo, trickling his dark eyes up the length of the bodies. "I've seen 'em with these." The younger detective ran a gloved finger through the colorful fletching of one of the arrows. "Used with old recurve bows."

"These kids want their full rides to AU. They wouldn't risk using that kind of weapon." Frank spoke in the flat, broad vowels of the Tohono O'odham people.

Arturo's sad, drooping eyes softened the otherwise hard lines of his face. "They're young and immortal. Nothing to risk and everything to gain from sending a message to the cartel."

"We'll see if prints turn up, but I'll talk with Graham and Russell to start.

They're the best, right?" Frank said, keeping his hunch about suspects other than high school kids warm in his thoughts.

*****

Frank raised a fist to knock, but the forensics lab door opened before he made contact.

"Poison," the tech reported.

"The arrowheads." Frank stated as much as asked.

"Paralyzed both victims." The tech handed Frank a multiple-page report confirming what the detective already suspected.

Frank flipped through the report, quickly scanning each page. "It's an old recipe."

The tech nodded. "Used for tribal warfare. Our people used it. So did the Mohaves, Apaches, and a few other tribes. No prints."

"I might've guessed. Thanks."

Frank wandered back to his office where two of the best archers on the reservation would be waiting for him.

*****

The two boys sat still in the waiting room of the Tohono O'odham Nation police headquarters. Though they shared some of the same bold features, the boys were opposites. Frank studied them through the blinds of his office window before calling them in.

A one-dimensional mohawk striped sixteen-year-old Graham Soto's skull. He rubbed his palms several times on the tops of his faded

25

jeans as if they were sweaty. Graham's broad physique overwhelmed a too-fitted white t-shirt.

A thick dark braid reached the middle of fifteen-year-old Russell Torres's spine. He wore a black t-shirt—featuring the name of a Tohono O'odham rock band—and jeans. On his feet were traditional Papago-style moccasins with missing beadwork here and there.

"Russell." Frank swept the boy into his office with serious eyes.

Russell entered and sat, bouncing the tips of his fingers on his thighs. The boy's thin fingers popping up and down reminded Frank of the boy's thin-light presence in general. He could imagine Russell barely tethered to gravity, moving along desert ground, perfectly formed for stalking other living creatures with a bow and arrow.

"How come I'm not in that room down the hall?" Russell asked.

Frank shook his head. "I knew your grandfather and your father. I don't need a special room for my questions." Frank could see the boy understood—he was more like an uncle interrogating him.

The detective leaned back in his chair. "You heard about what happened?"

Russell nodded. "It's why we're here, right?" His pogo-stick fingers finally rested as he stilled. "You think we did it."

Frank had chosen to break open dialogue with the boys through Russell because of candor like this. Graham appeared to have more of a presence than the smaller boy, but that was a default presumption.

Frank smiled. "I don't think you or Graham killed anyone. But maybe you know someone who's just as quick and just as accurate as you. Maybe someone who taught you how to make bows in the old way."

Frank nodded coaxingly while Russell focused on chewing the nail of an index finger. Frank couldn't tell if it was a nervous twitch or just a habit.

"What about your coach?" Frank tried not to notice the indicators of youth in the boy as this could distract him to an overly biased sympathy toward a child who also happened to be a suspect. Instead, he considered his own aging body with its extra rings of fat around his middle, arthritic joints and even the scars of injuries mapping time across his body.

Russell met Frank's gaze again. There was no surprise in the boy's eyes at Frank's unsubtle trap. "You know he was the first to get a full ride for archery in our district. And you know he's just as good, so why ask?" Russell straightened his posture, matching the confidence of his gaze.

"He never took his ride. He decided to stay in Rainmaker District and train up another generation. Your coach train you on live targets or bags and trees?"

Russell sighed through his nose. "Bags and trees and sometimes coyote and *Javelina*."

Frank leaned forward over his desk, a loud creak from his chair announcing his growing midsection and interest in the boy's responses. "So, at night—in the desert, with longbows?"

Russell nodded, compressing his lips.

"I've talked to some of the other coaches around the county, and none of them train that way."

It's legal."

"I didn't say it was illegal."

"He didn't do it."

"That's what I'm trying to discover for myself." The older boy would tell him the same, in more or less words. "What about poison arrowheads? He ever teach you any recipes?"

A tensed jaw muscle locked in defiance across Russell's broad features. "No."

The single word echoed against the boy's hardened expression of wide, immovable cheekbones and too-still eyes and lips. Frank knew the boy was telling the truth as far as he understood it, but he also knew Coach Emilio.

Emilio's grandfather was a shaman who knew how to make the arrowhead—the one used in war with the Apache that poisoned the River People. He also knew of Emilio's public anger at the drug traffickers.

"Go ahead and send Graham in."

27

Russell got up to leave but turned around. "Graham doesn't know anything either." The defiance lifted only long enough to slip his words past a still-clenched jaw.

He shut the door behind him before Frank could respond.

Frank leaned back in his chair, closing his eyes, then opening them to the darkness of reflection. Arturo would want to question the boys too. He would seed his questioning with a bias toward the outcome he wanted just as Frank had done, and he would still come up empty. If only the desert could talk. Frank would settle for questioning Emilio.

*****

Emilio Acuna sat in the last pew of St. Ignatius, his head down.

Behind Emilio, Frank smelled the air of the sanctuary, a lingering aroma of incense seducing his memory with images of his veiled mother entering the Confessional, her lips shaping the prayer born of the Virgin's fiat. St. Ignatius was less than a century old, built over the site of a Spanish mission that existed in the 1700s through the early nineteenth century. Mexican militia destroyed the old mission church as part of a forced claim on the southernmost territories of Arizona.

So many had tried to claim Papago lands.

St. Ignatius's priest, Father Jim Harris, was half Papago and respected in the community.

"Never thought I'd see you in here." The unhurried vowels of an indigenous speaker fringed with highbrow British turned Frank's and Emilio's heads. A sweet aroma of cigar smoke wafted from the cleric.

Father Harris stood up to his neck in black with a flash of white at his Adam's apple. His cassock gave his presence a somewhat medieval context. Like Frank, he wore his gray and white hair braided down his back.

Emilio crossed himself and rose, making his way to the other two men. "He's here for me."

The coach, squat-framed and muscular, had a natural amiability in his large dark eyes. Unlike the priest, his features were heavy and wide.

"Emilio needs to see me first." Father Harris's tea-colored eyes jested, his hitchhiker's thumb pointing back at the freestanding wooden box.

Frank grinned out of one side of his mouth. "Maybe I'll put my ear to the wood and get what I need."

"Render unto Caesar, *Padre*. I don't think I'll be long with the detective." Emilio lightly clapped the priest on his back.

"Can't promise that." The side smile disappeared.

Though the priest's eyes were serene, the amusement had expired on his face, a unique contortion in those parts of *Anglo* and American Indian with his dark skin and fine bone structure. "I'll be waiting."

Emilio followed Frank out of the church.

The two men were soon shrouded in a dry, desert wind, only interrupted in one instance by an all-too-intimate *sssss* of a snake. Frank noticed the glossy creature coiled under the bright yellow spray of Desert Marigold. Though it wasn't venomous, the reptile was a reminder to be alert for more dangerous species always on the move in the surface stillness of the Sonoran.

"I've known you as long as you've had breath," Frank began once they were a good distance away.

"Then you don't need to question me." Emilio stood in a wide stance, arms folded.

"I know you hate, and you have a bad temper. That's a lethal combination."

"Don't you get pissed off? The cartel uses our land for mule running and kidnaps our people for their drug fields and rapes our women. They make addicts out of the kids around here. They make it hard for us to pass through our own lands. Don't you have family down south? You ever see them? Maybe you put the poisoned arrows in those bastards. No one would question you—you have a badge to hide behind," Emilio accused.

The older man smiled inside at the passion in the younger man. His own passion had flattened with age, and he admired Emilio's, but he knew it was dangerous.

"My blood is old. It doesn't boil like yours. Just because I carry a gun doesn't mean I like to use it. Haven't shot an arrow in more than thirty years."

"So, you want to know where I was and who I was with and what I was doing and how I was doing it that night? Well, I was sleeping and you know as well as I do, I was doing it alone." Bitterness tinged Emilio's words. "Regina left for a white man in Silver." His face guarded his feelings well, but his tone didn't.

"Sorry. I knew you were separated. I hadn't heard the rest." Frank added a small frown to the naturally sympathetic droop at the outer corners of his eyes.

"I haven't told many people but figured you knew."

Though Frank felt sorry for Emilio, his mind scavenged for motive possibly buried in the emotion around a marriage breaking up. He hated suspecting a man he had known from as far back as his time in his mother's belly. "The poison we found on the arrows . . ." Frank paused to gauge Emilio's reaction.

Emilio frowned, but Frank couldn't tell whether it was a reaction to the talk about the younger man's failed marriage.

"He never taught me," Emilio answered Frank's half question, flattening his frown to a straight, serious lip line.

"Other than a couple of old women," Frank said, "you're the only one raised on the old ways."

"Even if he had taught me, anyone can look up that shit now," Emilio responded.

"But hate belongs to those who own it," Frank retorted.

Emilio straightened his posture, his highly defined body a single taut muscle. "Then we all own it here." Emilio kicked a rock he'd been moving around with his foot.

"Maybe." Frank looked at the pinkish stone suddenly and violently sprung, considering the anger behind the action.

Emilio shook his head. "You want a sacrificial lamb—not a suspect. I'm not a fucking lamb, but I'm not your wolf either."

"Can you take me to the militia?" Frank said, ignoring Emilio's defensive remark.

"We train with guns, not arrows, at the border."

"But a few are your former students?"

"I never taught anyone to hate."

"You don't have to—it's in your eyes."

Frank tried to forget the child he had known, looming behind the man who stood before him. He had survived on blind spots as a reservation detective. This was just one more blind spot he had to sustain through the life of a case.

"Meet me at the community center tomorrow at noon and I'll take you to a training."

"Are you preparing to defend the border or are you preparing for war?" Frank shouted as Emilio walked back toward the church.

Emilio spoke without stopping or turning around. "Both."

*****

Taken at face value, the San Felipe Gate didn't deserve the official status of gate as Frank had always thought. No more than a light pole, one guard, and a few pieces of barbed wire, it was the most naked part of the 1,969-mile U.S.-Mexico border. But now it wore the anger of eleven districts of Tohono O'odham. More than sixty men and women and a few teenagers who had come every other day for nearly a year to train for a battle that had thus far played out bloodlessly in their minds.

An elder just feet from the official border—which other than the single guard inside his booth, looked as lonely as a wire perimeter edging a ranch or farm—spoke to the militia in Spanish.

"Our Desert People passed like wind across this border for hundreds of years until the white man dropped a curtain so we might be divided—divided from family but never from our ancestors. We must become a stronger wind and be guided by the ancestors and most of all by *Se'ehe* in all of our movements . . ."

Frank understood, and visibly revered the man as he joined the crowd of armed men and women and several teenagers. He recognized many faces, including Graham's and Russell's.

Frank acknowledged other familiar faces with nods as he made his way over to where the boys stood off to the side of the other militia members near an ancient *saguaro* plant. "I thought you boys only shot arrows."

The boys remained serious despite a half smile pushing up one side of Frank's face.

"Plenty of kids their age here," Emilio said as he approached.

"What's that?" Frank pointed with his eyes at a figure off to the side of the militia gathering. He wandered toward a crude wire rendering of a person.

"The Martyr." Emilio shadowed Frank. "He's not the ghost of the man who killed those two traffickers because we don't know if he's still alive, but he's probably dead because those *narco* fuckers can find anyone. You wanna question him?" Emilio smiled, but Frank was serious staring into the soulless eyes, wondering if this case would wind up as empty.

"Who made it?" Frank asked.

Emilio pointed in the general direction of the militia. "All guilty."

"All archers too?" Frank spoke to The Martyr because his mind had not fully processed its existence, particularly in the context of the case.

Emilio shook his head. "About half. Half of those are shit and wouldn't know what to do with a longbow. About ten are good and four of those are kids. You've already talked to Graham and Russell."

Frank finally looked back at Emilio. "Give me the other eight then."

"You won't get your lamb here." Emilio's right hand moved to rest on a holstered gun at his side. It rested without the slightest twitch, but Frank took it as the younger man's show of protectiveness of his militia.

Frank looked back into The Martyr's unseeing eyes. "Let's see."

Emilio rejoined the group and whispered into the ear of a muscular Indian who stood at least a foot above everyone else. When Emilio stopped whispering, the large Indian moved toward Frank.

"I know you." Frank offered his hand, and the younger man accepted it, but his large brown eyes revealed a distrust the detective had seen often on the reservation. It was no more than a reflex, though.

"Your cousin is married to my cousin," the wall said.

Frank remembered. "You're Benito."

Benito nodded, the wariness lifting from his expression. "You wanna know where I was the night of the murder, right? I was sleeping at my girlfriend's house."

"How long has the militia been training?" Frank asked.

*****

Jennifer Leeper is an award-winning fiction author whose previous or forthcoming publications credits include *Poiesis, Aphelion Webzine, Cowboy Jamboree, The New Engagement, Alaska Quarterly Review, Falling Star Magazine* and *The Liguorian*. She has had works published by Alternating Current Press, Owl Canyon Press, Barking Rain Press, Whispering Prairie Press, Prensa Press and Spider Road Press.

The Poison of War is a mystery, published through Prensa Press. It spotlights the landscape of the American Southwest and Native American culture. This book is available on the following websites: Amazon, Thriftbooks, and Goodreads. Follow her on her facebook page: www.facebook.com/authorjenniferleeper.

3rd Place Winner   **Victoria Murata**

When the Mockingbird Won't Sing

Chapter One

June 1844, somewhere in the north Atlantic Ocean

The four-hundred ton, three-masted barque heaved its rigid 47 meters over each undulating wave, groaning with the swells of the Atlantic. A handful of passengers huddled on deck surrounding three bodies wrapped in sail cloth. Two women leaned into each other, tightening their shawls against the wet chill of the spray. A few crew scurried along the yards of the topsails high up, faint voices calling to each other. Burials at sea were commonplace, and the crew took little notice of the small group of mourners gathered below.

Four-year-old Biddy tilted her head back and looked up at the sails stretched taut against a blue sky scudded with rippled clouds. She breathed in the restorative sea air, so fresh after the stench down below where the more than two hundred passengers lived in close quarters. The large hand clutching her small one squeezed, and Biddy shifted her gaze to the sorrowful eyes of Mrs. Kelly.

"It's going to be all right, Dear."

Biddy wasn't sure what Mrs. Kelly was talking about, but she had been taught to respect her elders, so she smiled and nodded her head and squeezed back.

The ship's keel, the vessel's backbone, dipped into a trough and hauled itself back up. It provided the heaviest and strongest timbers in the ship, massive oak beams affording the greatest possible strength. This particular barque, the *Shenandoah,* had made the journey from England to America many times before, and this time was much like the others. Only the passengers were different.

Biddy stood near a man who droned the *De Profundis*, his voice competing with the waves crashing against the bow, the creaking of the larch planks on the frame of the hull, and the weeping of the women.

34

"If you, Lord, were to mark iniquities, who, O Lord, shall stand? But with you is forgiveness, that you may be revered. I trust in the Lord."

Biddy's light amber eyes regarded this man who wasn't a priest. She had always been a precocious child, and she perceived that not having a priest onboard was a source of concern for the passengers. She had overheard Annie Bell crying to a friend when her son had succumbed to ship fever.

"No doctor on board, and no priest. How will sweet Tommy ever get to Heaven?" and she had wrung her hands in despair.

"Don't you worry, Annie. The Lord knows Tommy's heart and He will welcome him through the pearly gates, rest assured," the friend had comforted, but that was small consolation to Annie. She knew that without a priest who would administer the Last Rites, her dear boy's soul would wander in Limbo forever. This was heartbreaking for her and for the mostly Irish Catholic passengers on board the *Shenandoah*, as family after family lost loved ones to ship fever.

The man droned on. "For with the Lord there is mercy, and with him is plenteous redemption. And he will redeem Israel from all his iniquities."

When the prayer ended, the mourners moved back as two men lifted one of the bundles to the ship's rail.

"May ye rest in peace Theresa Mary Hughes." The two men rolled the body over the side. Hardly a splash could be heard above the sound of wind and water.

Earlier that morning, Biddy had pleaded with her mother, but her mother's eyes were closed and she lay still. Finally, after sitting with her for awhile, Biddy had gone to Mrs. Kelly.

"Mam won't wake up," she had whined, "and I'm hungry."

Mrs. Kelly had sat her down and given her bread and a cup of water and had gone to check on her mother. When she came back, Biddy saw her speaking to a man in a low voice.

"The poor dear. She lost her father and brother just last week." The man had glanced at Biddy, and then nodded to Mrs. Kelly. Not much later, three wrapped bodies had been carried up to the deck, her mother among them.

Mrs. Kelly clutched Biddy to her, whether for warmth or comfort, the girl wasn't sure, but she was thankful for the closeness. As the ship rocked down into a swell and up again, a wave broke against the bow sending spray into the wind. It tugged golden strands of Biddy's hair from the disheveled plaits that had looked tidy days ago. The vibration of the ship as the waves pummeled the bow reminded Biddy of the figurehead attached to the prow. She remembered pointing to it when her family boarded the ship weeks earlier, and she wondered now who this woman was, and why she was fixed to the boat where she was being battered by waves and drenched in sea spray.

Biddy scrutinized two men hauling on a halyard through the jack-block close by, raising a lugsail. So many sails! After three days of calm, the captain was taking advantage of the brisk wind, and the crew scurried around the deck. As she observed the activity, she was hardly aware of another bundle rolling over the side and dropping into the ocean.

"May ye rest in peace, Conan Melvin Donovan."

An anguished cry from a mourner was in counterpoint to the joyful exclamation of a crewmember, happy to have the wind on his face and to be moving forward after being becalmed.

One body was left on the wet boards of the deck. The two men lifted it easily in its shroud, a lightness confessing to the wasted remains of its occupant.

"May ye rest in peace, Cathleen Bridget Murphy," and the body was rolled into the water just as the ship dipped into a trough.

Hearing her mother's name startled Biddy, and a vague but important apprehension registered in her four-year-old mind.

"Mama!"

She jerked her hand from Mrs. Kelly's and ran to the rail, pulling her small body up, searching the water. "Mama!" she cried, as she caught a glimpse of the brown dress her mother had worn every day, surrounded by the dark tumultuous water. Horrified, she saw her mother disappear beneath the surface as urgent hands grasped her from behind and pulled her back to the deck.

"She's gone, child. Say a prayer for your mother. She's in God's hands now."

"Mama! Mama!" Biddy cried, over and over, and the wind snatched her child's prayer and bore it up into the sky.

*****

Vicky Murata tells us her first novels grew out of a love of history and character and out of the question, *Would a character exhibit the same strengths and weaknesses in any situation and in any time period?* Her switch in genre from historical fiction to fantasy, gives multi-faceted answers. "For me, writing must satisfy my curiosity."

When the Mockingbird Won't Sing: True Grit in 1855, Oregon City is available in paperback, Kindle and audiobook form through Amazon. You can read more about Vicky on her facebook page and on her SouthWestwriters.com member page.

https://www.southwestwriters.com/author-pages-a-m/victoria-murata/

Honorable Mention **Edith Tarbescu**

One Will Three Wives

Chapter 1

Detective Cheri Marsh was accustomed to being pushed, jostled, and shoved. She was also used to the sounds of New York: tires screeching, horns blowing, and eardrum bursting construction. As she waited in line at the deli counter the woman behind her reeked of garlic. The man next to her smelled of cigarette smoke. It was dark outside and she could see people rushing to buses, subways, restaurants, bars. She planned to finish up at work, pick up her car with her gym bag inside and spend a couple of hours working out. She often told friends, "I don't miss Montana anymore," but that wasn't entirely true. She missed the mountains and the clean air. After she left Billings, Montana for Manhattan her grandmother told her, "Don't forget who you are and where you come from." She was too busy most of the time to think about who she was.

The woman in front of her couldn't decide what to order. The garlic lady was breathing down her neck and Mr. Tobacco was gulping mouthfuls of air next to her. While the deli kept filling up a woman in back shouted, "Let's go."

As Cheri inched forward she stopped thinking about Montana and thought about food. After finally ordering black coffee and two pastries, she made her way outside. She noticed the cloud-filled sky and took a deep breath. It smelled like snow. Wending her way through the crowds, she realized she wasn't a newbie anymore and elbowed a few stragglers out of her way.

Standing in front of the 20th precinct on West 82nd Street, Cheri inhaled deeply. Most people were home from work by now. She and her partner still had work to do

* * *

38

She passed the Snapple machine in the lobby, the receptionist behind a glass partition and the elevator before she ran up three flights of stairs to the detectives' squad room. It sounded like Grand Central Terminal: phones ringing, people arguing, detectives barking orders but Cheri stayed focused on her computer. She only looked up when she heard, "Bullshit, you're kidding me." That's when she noticed her partner, James, making his way through the maze. She shouted "O'Brien, where were you?"

"I decided to make a food run." He caught her eye and smiled. She managed a half-assed smile but he didn't seem to notice. She handed him a bag from the deli on Broadway. He pulled out a flaky, still-warm apple turnover. "My favorite. Thanks."

"Figured you needed this after your bout with the flu." He was only an inch taller than her, but his broad shoulders made him appear bigger than five-ten. His dark hair was his best feature. While they were dating Cheri teased him about having a Samson complex. Now, she tried to avoid looking at him. But she always knew when he was near, his after-shave cologne was a give-away.

They finished at the same time and walked out together. "Have a good one," he said.

"You, too." She turned and walked away, determined not to look back.

She was at the gym less than ten minutes when her cell rang. She picked it up on the first ring and recognized the Captain's voice. "Work," he grunted. "You have to take over a case from McClure and Casey."

She was tempted to say, Now? Instead she said, "Yes, sir. But what's the story with the other team?"

"They'll explain. Call your partner. Here's the address, tell him where to meet you. And get moving."

She alerted James then ran down a flight of stairs, picked up her precinct pool car, a white Chevy Impala, and drove straight to the crime scene.

As soon as she jumped out of the car she spotted her partner. James was standing inside the perimeter of the yellow police tape in a huddle with Detectives McClure and Casey along with a couple of cops in uniform. Techs were working the scene nearby. Crowds of onlookers were craning their necks, trying to take photos with Smartphones as the policemen kept ordering them to step back. The crowd kept pressing forward, calling out questions. Cheri noticed a reporter from the Daily News, but she didn't respond when he called her name.

"Looks like we're playing sloppy seconds," James whispered.

Cheri nodded. She noticed the Forensics' team and the Coroner's team at work on the body. She recognized some of those people but didn't stop to interrupt them. Flashbulbs were popping as Detective Bill McClure pointed to the body on the ground. "Either suicide or a homicide. Fifth floor, balcony."

James scanned the side of the building then faced the outgoing detectives. "That height is definitely a ball breaker. Fill us in."

"We will," said McClure. "Meanwhile, I want you to know that everything's been bagged and tagged. We're handing over a clean case."

"We didn't ask to get taken off the case," said Casey. "We got fucked on account of me." He let out a whoosh of air and moved closer to Marsh and O'Brien. "After we discovered the vic's last name, it rang a bell but not right away. Plus, his name isn't uncommon in New York: Rabinowitz."

Cheri nodded. "Who's the vic?"

"A hedge fund manager. My wife works at his brokerage firm, back office. Conflict of interest according to the captain when I told him about my wife's job."

"Luck of the Irish," said James.

"Yeah, " said Casey.

"Any witnesses?" asked Cheri.

McClure shrugged. "Not so far. We canvassed the buildings across the street, nobody saw or heard anything. We were specifically interested in the person who lives in the apartment across from the vic. We went over there little while ago, heard noise inside so we kept banging on the door. No response. Could've been a radio or TV turned on to deter burglars. Name of the woman who owns the condo is Helen Powers. A widow. Lives alone. Got that info from a neighbor."

"We'll get on it," said Cheri. She and James turned and looked at the body lying on the ground. As she stared at the mix of dried blood and brains spilled on the sidewalk, she wondered if the vic jumped or was pushed. Her gut feeling told her he was shoved. Hard. She was learning to trust her instincts but she needed more than a hunch to call it homicide.

"All the stuff in the apartment's been bagged," said Casey. "Forensics is still checking for fingerprints."

Marsh and O'Brien watched as the coroner's team wearing latex gloves carefully turned the body over, exposing more dried blood. "If he was going to take a flyer," she told James, "why was he all dressed up? Expensive leather shoes, fancy suit, gold cufflinks." She bent closer and noticed that he was still wearing a gold and silver Rolex so probably wasn't a robbery. She made notes then told the people working the crime scene that she and O'Brien were going upstairs to check out the apartment.

She faced McClure and Casey. "After we check out the possible witness across the street, we'll notify next of kin."

"That part's tricky," said McClure. "There was a will in the top drawer of the desk with a note: If anything happens to me, notify my attorney. He will sort it out with my wife and two ex-wives. There was a name and numbers for his attorney. We called his cell earlier. According to him, one of the wives lives on the Upper East Side. The other one lives at 18 Gramercy Park."

McClure handed her the pad with the names and address jotted down. "Third wife lives in Rio."

"As in Rio de Janeiro?"

Detective Casey winked at her. "You got it."

McClure handed over the keys to the victim's apartment. "Any questions, call. "

"Will do," said James.

"Let's check out the apartment upstairs," said Cheri.

They took the elevator to the fifth floor and Cheri opened the door to a huge, at least for New York, living room with big windows and a balcony at the other end of the room. As soon as they entered the room, she eyed the furniture: white leather couches, a well-stocked bar, an antique desk. No paintings, no personal photographs.

They each put on a pair of latex gloves and started going through the evidence that had been bagged and tagged by Detectives McClure and Casey. Not only were there bags of pot but also cocaine and a silver spoon for sniffing. "No ordinary spoon for a hedge fund manager," said Cheri. She checked the name on the back of the spoon, but it didn't mean anything to her.

James sniffed the coke. "Good stuff," he murmured.

"Put it back," she said jokingly, then added, "But if it's that good we could sell it on the street."

He laughed as she continued going through sealed evidence bags. "Hey, look at this." She handed him a business card that read: ESCORT SERVICE on one side and MASSEUSE on the other, then told him that the note from McClure said this was found on top of the desk in the room leading to the balcony.

James whistled loud. "We'll interview the woman from the escort service as soon as possible. Anything else of interest in that evidence bag?"

She took her time going through the bags one by one sifting through everything. When she was on the next to last bag she shouted, "James, c'mere." She held out her hand. "Take a look at this."

"It's a receipt. But what's it for?" he asked.

Her face turned red with excitement. "It's for a custom-made suit. Ready for pick up next week."

James took the receipt from her and studied it. "Jeez, the guy really had big bucks." He thought for a second. "But a guy doesn't order a thirty-eight hundred dollar suit if he's planning to kill himself."

Cheri nodded. "You got it. The case has all the markings of a homicide now." She shook her head and chuckled . "We should call it the Custom-Made Suit Case from now on."

James looked at her and smiled. From the look in his eyes, she was glad he appreciated her tight jeans and blue turtleneck.

"More luck of the Irish with this receipt," he said. "Guard it carefully."

"I'm gonna sleep with it."

McClure and Casey stuck their heads in the door. "One more thing," said Casey. "We checked out the security camera in the lobby. The tape is missing."

"Did you talk to the superintendent?" asked Cheri.

"Yup," said McClure. "Just before you arrived on the scene."

"What did he say?" asked James.

"Said, that's Nueva York."

"Might have been tampered with," said McClure.

"Gotcha," said James. "We'll check it out."

"How about fingerprints?" asked Cheri. "Any prints?"

McClure turned and looked at her. "It's early, but so far only those of the deceased, a middle-age man named Benjamin Rabinowitz, partner in a hedge firm according to his business card. You'll get the examiner's full report when it's ready, could take time. They usually do."

"Outer door found open or locked?" asked Cheri.

Detective Casey turned away from the window and said, "The police on the scene found the door locked. Looks like you can secure it from the inside if you're leaving. You don't need a key."

Cheri nodded as she faced her partner. "If he wasn't pushed maybe he was pretending to be Spiderman."

James nodded. "Anything can happen in New York."

McClure told them that he and Casey were leaving and the four detectives shook hands. "Jeez, I hate to leave this case," said Casey, turning to leave. "Going to be a whopper."

As Cheri continued looking through the evidence bags, she found the copy of the will and held it up to show her partner."

"One will, three wives," said James, reading the note from McClure attached to it. "Hope the guy made tons of money."

"You ever hear of a poor hedge fund manager?"

He laughed then raised his arm and sneezed into his elbow. "Excuse me,"

She took a step back. "Hope you're over the flu."

"I'm over it but still a little shaky."

Cheri nodded as she untied her pony tail and let her hair hang loose. When she first told James she was part Native-American he said, "You're pulling my leg." She finally showed him pictures from a family reunion. Half her relatives looked German-American like her father. The other half looked Assiniboine like her mother's family in Montana. She inherited the Germanic genes: blonde hair with blue almond shaped eyes.

She looked at the pad of paper again. "Casey or McClure jotted down the names and addresses of the wives for us."

James smiled as he ran his fingers through his hair. "Wonder why one of the wives lives in Rio."

"We ought to fly down there to interview her," said Cheri.

James raised his eyebrows. "The Captain's not going to spring for a trip to Samba-ville," he said. "We'll have the Rio Leos talk to her first. If she becomes a person of interest, we might make the trip. Meanwhile, I'll visit one of the women. You talk to the other one. That okay with you?"

"I like checking out expensive cribs. We should also drive down to Wall Street and talk to the dead man's partner at the hedge fund as soon as we can. But you're the boss."

He sneezed into his elbow again. "I agree. We also need to find out about the three wives: motives, alibis..." He popped a cough drop in his mouth.

She nodded. "Everybody can use extra dough. But money wouldn't be the only motive. You heard of revenge, haven't you?" Luckily, he didn't appear to take it personally. Jesus what was wrong with her? She kept putting her foot in her mouth lately.

He rubbed his jaw thoughtfully. "Just had a funny thought, maybe the guy on the balcony was an actor doing publicity for a show before someone saw it and didn't like his act. Speaking of the theater, I have an in with a scalper. He can get me two seats center orchestra, any show you want. to see." Wearing a pair of latex gloves, he continued going through the plastic evidence bags, not looking at Cheri while he spoke.

44

She didn't look at him, either. "I'm kind of busy these days," she said, trying to sound as casual as possible then quickly added, "Can I get back to you?"

"Sure, no problem. Sorry to digress. We have to talk to the lawyer and get the date of the latest will and find out which of the women stands to inherit the whole enchilada. Three wives?" James repeated. "Randy bastard. Probably deserved to take a flyer over a balcony."

"A flyer as in murdered," said Cheri. She pulled a Kleenex out of her jeans pocket and rubbed her eyes. They felt dry from the cold air. "About the theater tickets, I appreciate you asking. I am seeing somebody. Besides, those tickets would be expensive."

She reminded herself to use will power or she'd find herself in the same fix. She and James weren't living together at the time, but they were becoming serious, especially after three years. Besides she believed in "Duty First" as if it was one of the Ten Commandments. She also had to be careful. As a former actor, she knew the inside of the unemployment office.

"The police in Rio been alerted yet?" he asked.

Cheri turned to look at her partner. "Casey told me he spoke to them earlier, said we should get a call back from them." She stared at a picture of the dead man lying on the ground. The photo was gruesome. Five stories weren't high but even with a helmet, sidewalks were capable of breaking more than a few bones. In the other photos the guy was covered with a white sheet. She continued thinking about the victim. "A Wall Street wheeler-dealer," she said, facing James. "I bet more than a few people wanted to see this dude laid out in concrete. "Maybe a drug dealer took him out," she added. "Brokers are big users."

"Really? That's news to me," he said with a smirk as he studied the names and addresses of the wives. He turned and looked out of the window. "Looks like snow. We better get moving " He glanced at the pad with the wives' names again. I'll notify Kati. You give Leslie the news. We'll talk to Brazil later or tomorrow. First, we should try to interview the person across the street. It's getting late, maybe somebody's home by now."

"It's a deal," said Cheri. "Let's lock up first." She pulled a woolen beret out of one of her coat pockets and a pair of woolen gloves out of the other.

When they got downstairs they found the coroner's team and the forensics team still at work. "We'll be transporting the body to the morgue soon," the coroner told Cheri. "That's what the crowd is waiting for, then they'll disperse. I swear New Yorkers are hungry for blood."

"You have our cell numbers," said Cheri. ""We're going across the street, hope to talk to a potential witness." As O'Brien and Marsh turned to cross the street, she got a blast of cold air coming off the Hudson River. One of her favorite walks in New York, when it isn't bitter cold, was along the embankment between the West Side Highway and the river. During the summer she loved watching sailboats meander upriver, along with barges and power boats.

They stopped in front of the apartment building across the street and looked up. "This is it," said Cheri. "Not sure this woman will be of much help. Look at the distance between this building and the vic's apartment across the street. You'd need binoculars."

"We'll see," said James.

.

*****

Edith Tarbescu is the author of the mystery *ONE WILL: THREE WIVES* which was the winner of the New Mexico-Arizona Book Awards for 2022 in the category of Best Fiction E-Books. Her memoir, *Beyond Brooklyn*, will be out soon. She is also a produced playwright.

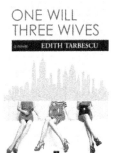

One Will: Three Wives was published in 2020 by Adelaide Books. This mystery is available in print and ebook form through Amazon. You can follow Edith through her facebook page or her member page at www.southwestwriters.com.

Honorable Mention   **Jodi Lee Stewart**

Canyon of Doom

Chapter 1 – The Stranger

I laughed when a two-hundred-pound sheep threw me off his back when I was five. I cried when they told me I couldn't get back on.

Losing the Woolly Ride competition at the Navajo Nation Fair wasn't what upset me. I just didn't like that sheep thinking he'd pulled something over on me.

Someone could say he pulled the wool over my eyes, and I'd laugh at the play on words, but I wouldn't think it was funny deep inside. I don't like being fleeced. Oh, sorry. What I'm trying to explain is how the stranger who came to our Navajo Rez that hot day in early August threw my suspicious-sensing nature into high alert.

As it turns out, I was right on target.

It wasn't that the stranger was too tall to be Navajo. So was my grandfather. The stranger's starched and pressed Levi jeans weren't the problem either. The Marines in our family wore their jeans all perfect like that too.

No, something else about the tall man didn't add up. I decided that right after we collided on the sidewalk by the Bashas' Grocery Store parking lot in my town of Mesa Redondo. The collision was kind of my fault since I didn't look very well before taking off in a run toward Copper Park. Okay, I didn't look at all. My mind was on important things, like catching Cousin TeeShirt and coaxing a barrel-racing lesson out of him later that afternoon.

I remember glancing over my shoulder at Auntie Blue Corn at the flea market the same moment I took off and wham! I slammed dead center into what felt like a sack of concrete. It changed my perspective, that's for sure.

Sparkles in the cement and a sno-cone holder flattened by a black shoeprint loomed large on my way down to the sidewalk in a perfect belly flop. On impact, my air whistled out with an airy ssshrrrshh, followed by a curly wheeze. My whole body burned, and for the first time in four days, I forgot how much I missed my best friend, Birdie.

While I struggled to get a deep breath, boots and shoes gathered around me, and I hated that because it meant I was the center of attention for all the wrong reasons. Sharp-toed brown cowboy boots covered in bumpy leather almost speared my arm.

"You all right, young lady?" rumbled a thunderbolt kind of voice I didn't recognize. I looked up, then rocked my head backward to get my first glimpse of the stranger.

"I-I guess so," I stammered.

"You sure?" There was that cavernous voice again. Heat pricked my cheeks and spread to my ears. Could I just blink and disappear?

I sat up. The man thrust an arm toward me. He cleared his throat, impatiently, I thought. I wasn't used to grasping a stranger's hand, but it seemed my best escape from the circle of gawkers.

My hand no more than touched his when I found myself sailing off the ground as fast as a whip snap. He leaned down close to my face. Eyes the exact amber-brown color of Tiger's Eye gems glared at me over a pair of mirrored sunglasses.

"Don't run through crowds." His voice made me think of a low dog growl. He walked off in long steps and vanished into the crowd. I stared at the spot where he'd become air.

Oh-my-gosh! Birdie was missing everything—fame because our picture was in the newspaper, the last few weeks before school started, and a stranger of interest in town.

Before the day was over, Birdie would also miss the most dangerous day

*****

Jodi Lea Stewart is a fiction author who writes about the triumph of the human spirit through overcoming adversity. Her lifetime friendship with an eclectic mix of all races, cowpunchers, country folks, intellectuals, as well as the southern *gentry*, inspires Jodi to write historical and contemporary novels set in the South, the Southwest, and beyond.

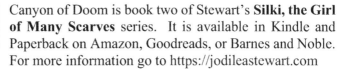

Canyon of Doom is book two of Stewart's **Silki, the Girl of Many Scarves** series. It is available in Kindle and Paperback on Amazon, Goodreads, or Barnes and Noble. For more information go to https://jodileastewart.com

Section Two

Opening Chapter of an UN-Published Book

If an author really wants to understand the strengths and weaknesses in their writing, they need reviewers who are able to give them constructive critiques. All of the pieces in this section are books which are finished, but not yet published. They are undergoing the final process of reviews and editing. This category allows beginners to practice their skills while not competing with long time professionals.

As in the previous chapters, all entrants are allowed to request the review information and suggestions from the judging staff on what works and what doesn't.

First Place   **Paul Knight & Chris Allen**

Overture

Chapter One

In a whitewashed, thatched roof cottage in the Irish countryside, Ryan Reilly lay in his bed, perched on the edge of consciousness. His mind created a cavernous concert hall. Every seat was filled, with people jostling for positions along the walls. He placed himself at the podium, scanning the orchestra below, poised to play, awaiting his direction. As he raised the baton, the audience froze, speech was suspended as anticipation surged throughout the theater. The wand sliced through the air, initiating a symphony. Waves of notes, quavering and lyrical, flowed around the listeners causing them to wrap their arms around their bodies and sway in ecstasy.

With every sweep of his arms, vibrations from the imagined instruments seeped from his mind into his bedroom. Objects around him rattled, and a faint blue glow, like mist over a moonlit lake, filled the room. As the instruments boomed to a crescendo, more objects bounced and danced until a glass phoenix, wings outstretched, tumbled from a shelf above his bed and crashed onto a table. The noise of the impact shattered the music like the crystal shards that now peppered his bedroom. He sat upright, clutching the blankets. Curling his chin into his chest, he sucked air Into his lungs, letting it out through pursed lips, forcing his heart to slow its rhythm. He lay back against the pillow, stretching his arms and hands to release tension.

*****

On a planet mottled with blue continents and red oceans more than a hundred light years from Earth, a solitary technician sat inside a dimly lit room of the Protectorate, staring at flickering numbers and shifting graphs that scrolled across a battery of giant screens. He preferred the night shift when the world was quiet. What better time to monitor the displays that tracked the activity of music, both beneficial and nefarious, across the universe.

Nestled among the screens was a small unassuming display, older than anyone in the building. For generations it remained static and silent, waiting to report the single piece of information it was designed to capture. The technician barely noticed when it activated with a rapid series of flashing graphs. Focusing on the images, he gasped.

"It can't be," he whispered. Scooting his chair to face it and sliding his hands across the controls, he double checked the data. Triangulating the signal, he paused, his eyes widening. It was from Earth, the birthplace of all music in the universe. It was the strongest emission he had ever seen or had ever heard about. Alarm bells sounded in his head. Springing from his chair, he rushed down a long hallway lined with images of revered composers: Johann Sebastian Bach, Ludwig von Beethoven, John Williams, Pyotr Tchaikovsky. "Please be there," he muttered, hoping his supervisor, Dr. Sha, was still working in her office.

The door was slightly open, and he burst through, shedding the decorum required of him when speaking to a superior. "It's happened. The Prime Monitor." He paused before the stately woman seated behind a translucent desk. Catching his breath, he reiterated, "The Prime Monitor. I've never seen anything like it. It's set to display only if there is a Level One."

Sha assessed the face of the man before her. It was swirling with splashes of reds and oranges indicating great excitement.

"Dr. Sha, it must be a One, right?"

"Bless the Protectors. We haven't seen a Level One in over 200 years. How long was the signal?"

"Barely an instant. I almost missed it."

"Could the Abductors have seen it? If they did, they will mobilize everything they have to grab a Level 1."

She leaned forward toward the amber button on the corner of her desk. Her finger trembled slightly from anticipation. Or was it apprehension? When she pushed the button, the staccato beat of a snare drum reverberated throughout the building, alerting those working the night shift. "Go back to your station, Liel. We have a lot of work ahead."

As the door slid shut behind him, her long fingers drummed out a message on her panel, relaying what had occurred and ending with "It is imperative we get there first."

*****

Paul Knight, a consulting biologist, has written hundreds of technical reports and published numerous articles on natural history. His true passion, however, is writing sci-fi and fantasy stories. He is currently working on three novels; one about music, another involving archaeology, and the third centered around mysterious photos documenting prehistory.

Co-Author, Chris Allen, is a retired archaeologist who started writing short stories in 2014. Since then, she has won awards for storytelling and editing. Her latest book, *Alchemy's Reach*, co-authored, will be published in 2023. This is the first of several awards she accumulated in this contest.

Second Place   **Jonathan Seyfried**

Paradigm Shift

Chapter 1
1996

He's right on the mountain's edge.

The veins on Naz's forearms twine around strands of muscle, providing the lifeblood needed to power his handstand. The city sprawls behind him. Albuquerque's lights glimmer against the sky at dusk. His orange shirt tumbles down and I notice the tight ridges of his abdomen. Lately, this summer, when guys take off their shirts, I've found myself staring. No, I don't want to touch Naz that way, because he's my cousin. But I do want to *be* him: drinking life in big gulps, handstanding on a cliffside. Maybe one day I'll be able to act on the world the way Naz does. I'm twelve and he's seventeen, so I've got five years to learn how to handstand and to flick off my fear. Even as I entertain this hope, the hopelessness of it gives me a sinking feeling. Acting on the world feels out of reach because I'm not the kind of person who leaps into anything. Somehow I need to figure out how to stop being so shy. Then I can learn how to handstand.

"Naz, you're being an idiot. Again!" Izzy shouts although she smiles afterward. He never listens to her. We all know that Izzy scolds him just to put her disapproval on the record in case they get into trouble later. There have already been more than five scoldings as we hiked up the mountain and we all expect there to be plenty more. It's how they relate to each other. She says, "Let's go. We're late."

Izzy and I are the same age, but we go to different schools. Before my brother was born, all of us cousins were going to have names that start with I. From the start, my aunt and uncle called Ignacio and

Isabel by their nicknames Iggy and Izzy. I've always been just Ian. In 5th Grade, though, Ignacio decided to become Naz, and then my parents named my brother Jacob after my mom's best friend who died of AIDS in 1991.

Naz slowly lowers his legs back to the ground. I exhale and wipe my palms on my shorts. Even though it's cooler up here at the Sandia's crest, the uncomfortable July heat still gets to me. A bead of sweat travels down my spine. I'm not terrified of heights, but Naz's stunts up here make my heart pound. Playing at the edge of death has never been my game. I don't think I've ever taunted anything, and definitely not a straight plummet hundreds of feet down to a pit of sharp boulders.

Naz wiggles his torso in order to get the rumpled shirt to slide back down. He hops and then lets out a long hoot. "The aliens are watching, right? So let's give 'em a show."

Izzy says, "As if! Like the aliens care what you do."

Over the last week, every conversation gets around to this eventually. I wonder what my teachers would have said if President Clinton's announcement had come during the school year and how they would have kept the class under control while all the crazy speculation let loose. I watch the network news every weeknight and all the government has said so far is that multiple radio telescopes around the world picked up a signal transmitted from the neighborhood of the Arcturus star system. The officials keep repeating that no aliens are here – it's a signal from far away. But that hasn't stopped the militia and cult people from stockpiling ammo. My teachers would definitely repeat something they say to us a lot about the end of the Cold War: it's a new historical era. My social studies teacher even showed us a book she had bought in 1992 called *The End of History*. So, with alien contact happening now, the world is probably going to change all over, yet again.

Jake emerges from behind some shrubs back toward the trail. "Ian, didn't mom tell us that we were supposed to be back by sunset?"

I walk toward him. "Would you please stop wandering off? Plus, you missed something totally awesome. Naz did a handstand right on the side of the cliff."

Jake's eyes widen.

Izzy says, "Like a moron. Let's go."

"Wow," Jake says as we start to head back to the trail.

Naz runs from the cliff's edge to catch up with us at the start of the trail heading back down. After tucking his hair behind his ears, Naz smiles. When he smiles, he looks like a swarthy pirate. "Relax, sis. That was like, what, my thousandth handstand?"

When I look at Naz, I see a kind of beautiful energy that only a few guys his age possess. I haven't told anyone yet, but I've known for a while that I'm different. Well, there are a lot of ways I'm different, but one of the important ways is that my crushes aren't what they are supposed to be. At night, when I am drifting off to sleep, I imagine all the dates I would go on with a boy at my school or, in moments less connected to reality, dates with the 90210 actor Jason Priestley. The details of how I end up at the mall or on a hike with my future boyfriend are never really clear. I have no idea how it will happen. I just enjoy imagining time with someone who will help me experience the world the way that Naz does when we four cousins are together. Naz is the ideal outgoing teenage boy: aggressive but always kind. He's pure adventure. Hesitation just never seems to occur to him.

A bead of sweat travels down Naz's temple and he wipes it when it gets to his cheek. Loose hairs on his head drift with the light evening wind. As we start down the trail, the mountaintop breeze feels good, and I stretch my arms into the air. Naz runs over and grabs my hands. He tries to twirl me around but I'm too big for that now. I wriggle free and push him away.

Naz says, "Aw, Ian, I almost got you. Come here, Jake!" Then my brother sees that Naz wants to catch him, so Jake runs down the trail ahead of us. Naz bounds after him.

Izzy and I watch as they run around a corner in the trail, passing out of our sight. A boulder blocks our view of them. Izzy and I make our way down, in no rush. This segment of the trail returns us to the cliffside. We round the boulder and find Jake standing still. It's a weird stillness like he's frozen. Then Jake raises his arm, pointing to our left. I turn my attention to follow where Jake points. There's nothing there, just the edge of the trail right on the cliff's edge. Beyond the edge, you can see the streetlights of the curvy streets of Albuquerque's northeast heights.

"Wait, where's Naz?" Izzy asks.

I think I am the first to figure it out. The knowledge of it arrives halfway. The other half of the knowledge remains stuck in a fog. I start trembling as I walk to the edge of the trail. I kneel down, the tiny pebbles of the trail dimpling my knees. I put my hands on the line of rocks that form the edge.

Jake says, "He tripped."

I can hear Izzy screaming but the sound feels surprisingly distant. I lean forward so that I can see over the edge. Hundreds of feet below, almost at the center of this one oval-shaped boulder, I see him. In the dusk, from this far up, that oval boulder looks like an eye with an orange pupil in the middle. That orange is Naz's shirt.

*****

At Naz's funeral, all the adults in my family have allergy-season eyes: baggy, red, seeping. During the pastor's eulogy, Izzy holds my right hand. In my other hand, I hold Jake's. According to my parents, I have to be in charge of Jake for a while because a five-year-old can't understand what's really going on.

The pastor looks like a retired football player. My aunt and uncle weren't religious and so they chose this pastor based on a recommendation. Everything about the day of Naz's funeral runs too quickly for me to keep my attention focused. Just being in the presence of such sadness overwhelms my senses. I can barely look at my aunt and uncle. As they walk to their place in the church pew next to us they hobble with unsure steps. My aunt hunches over with her head down, curling into the embrace of my grandmother. My uncle has developed a strange look: his right eye is constantly open wider than the left.

The service begins with a few short speeches. There's a huge picture of Naz below the pulpit. It's his last school picture, with the standard blue background. He wore a maroon button shirt with a weirdly large collar. He left the top three buttons unbuttoned to show off the necklace he got from a vendor at Venice Beach during our family trip last summer. From a distance, it seems like a crucifix, but up close you could see that it was a sword with a dragon wrapped around it. He gave it to me when he got tired of it. It's in my pocket now.

When I study the photograph of Naz, I can just make out the line of definition that extended from the bottom of his neck marking the division of the muscles of his upper chest.

At one point, the pastor says, "Physical death is just an event. Ignacio Martinez knew Jesus and therefore will be united with every Christian that knew him."

My mother, sitting on the other side of Jake, gasps. She whispers to my father just loud enough so that I am able to overhear it: "What a jerk."

My father takes her hand in both of his and rubs it slowly. His arm hair pokes out around his cuffs.

The funeral concludes with one of my aunt's friends, a woman with big hair, reading a poem. It's a Christian poem that mentions Jesus a lot while also talking about soaring doves and ocean waves. I can't make sense of what the poem is trying to say.

The reception takes place in the large lobby of the church, which has the same style of furniture as the lobby of my uncle's law firm.

As I wander around eavesdropping, every conversation seems to be about the aliens. It's messed up that people just can't stop talking about it, even at a funeral. Although, I have to admit that I'm also guilty of obsessing about the Signal. Yesterday the government announced that the Signal contains much more information than they originally thought. In the days since Naz died, I've spent as much time in the library as I can, reading every news article that I find about it. The smartest people on the planet have been trying to make sense of how the world has changed, but all that's known for now is that the Signal contains an unfathomable amount of data. They're trying to translate it but haven't been able to make sense of anything yet.

Several of the articles mentioned an idea called "paradigm shift." They said that the alien signal will bring a new paradigm shift for all of humanity. I asked the librarian to help me find out where that phrase came from. The philosopher Thomas Kuhn had invented the concept of paradigm shift but he's not writing any of the newsmagazine essays about the alien signal because he died from lung cancer a few weeks before Naz.

A paradigm shift happens when a new discovery redefines all of science and everything we think about the universe suddenly changes.

With Naz suddenly gone, my own personal paradigm is shifting too. What's weird, though, is that I can spend hours at a time pretending that Naz is still alive. I can't believe how easy it is: thinking about Nazy being alive fits so comfortably into a ready-made groove. When I try to imagine a world without Naz in it, that's what feels fake.

Someone grabs my hand, and I turn to see Izzy. Her brown eyes glisten. I think she's gotten taller than me and I hadn't noticed that until now.

"Come with me."

She leads me away from the reception and down a hallway further into the church. On the walls, there are large framed photographs of a very attractive young man dressed up to look like Jesus. In several of them, his robes hang loosely open to display a smooth and well-defined torso.

Izzy leads me into a large office. The pastor, standing behind his desk, says, "You must be Ian. I'm Pastor Greg."

I attempt to speak, but my throat is phlegmy. I cough and then say, "Nice to meet you. Thanks for doing the funeral."

Izzy lets go of my hand and shoves me toward Pastor Greg. "Listen to what he says."

Pastor Greg laughs and walks around to the front of his desk. He sits on the edge. "I'd really like for both you and Izzy to join the Youth Group here at Desert Renewal. I think you would get a lot out of it.

Especially in those middle school years when it can be so tough. You'll have a group of people your age who will be there for you."

"We'll be there, Pastor Greg," Izzy says.

I'm trying to figure out what to say. Obviously, I'm not going to go anywhere near this youth group because this church is infamously anti-gay and I spend every night imagining what it's like to kiss various boys. As I start to try to come up with an excuse, I wonder if I should just come out to Izzy. Then I realize adding a surprise like that on top of everything probably would not be a considerate thing to do. Keeping my secret is stressful enough and I don't want to burden her with it. Several celebrities have come out recently and their announcements always send their loved ones through a difficult process. This is not the right time.

"He's shy," Izzy says.

"No big deal." Pastor Greg then gives me a gentle smile. "Whenever you are ready, Ian, we'll be here for you, to bring you closer to Jesus."

My eyes widen. The bold religiosity feels creepy to me. I manage to say, "I need to find my brother. I'm in charge of him."

Izzy stares at me, waiting for me to say I'll go to the youth group. She rubs her right eyebrow, near the small birthmark on her temple.

"I'll talk with you later," I say as I leave and head back down the hallway with the sexy Jesus photos.

I weave through a few clusters of adults. One person says, "...worry about it. If they wanted to be here, they'd already be here."

In another cluster, a high-pitched voice says, "God's image, right? It will be interesting to see how they handle not being so special anymore."

I find Jake slumped in a chair near a wall that is made entirely of rectangular windows. His eyes are half-closed.

"Hey, buddy," I say as I sit in the chair next to him.

"When are the aliens going to get here?"

"I don't know. No one knows."

"Naz would have liked meeting the aliens." Jake leans his head to the side as he curls into the chair.

I look out the window. The church is on a big street and cars drive by pretty much in a constant stream. They go by, entering and exiting my sight: zoom, zoom, zoom.

"Naz liked meeting everyone, buddy."

*****

Jonathan Seyfried (they/them) is a former history teacher living in Albuquerque. Jonathan's previous short fiction and novels include the *Time Riven* trilogy. They have created a podcast, *A Socialist Reads Atlas Shrugged,* and a BookTok series, *Out of Print.* As a queer and nonbinary writer of fantasy and speculative fiction, Jonathan loves creating genderqueer worlds.

Third Place   **Joe Cappello**

The White Ace

Chapter 1 – Shame on Ralphie

Ralphie Licastro had a bad case of the willies. It started as a burning sensation in the pit of his stomach, rumbling like a volcano about to expel his lunch in one of only two possible directions. He made a half-hearted attempt to hustle out to second base when his friend, Mario Briosch, yelled at him to get the lead out of his ass. Every time he said that, Ralphie instinctively ran his hand over his backside. He knew there wasn't any lead, but feared the willies might have surreptitiously taken revenge on his bottom prompting the comment. He didn't need a new wrinkle added to the long list of wrinkles that had already plagued him throughout his grammar school years. He'd gotten razzed for resembling the skinny kid in those comic book ads who got sand kicked in his face. Or, teased for hair that wouldn't stay put no matter how much goo he heaped on it. Or, mocked for a white shirt that stuck out of his Valley of Tears uniform trousers no matter how many times he tucked it in. He didn't want to add his backside to the list of things the kids in his class, especially the girls, could snicker at when he passed them.

Ralphie's friends wanted the lead comment to shake him up, keep him on his toes for the punch ball games they played at recess. He had the best of intentions, wanting to play well, help his team win. But he couldn't help imaginary scenarios from unfolding in his mind, carrying him to other places like a kite in response to unpredictable gusts of wind. Last week, he missed a line drive during a game while wondering if the nuns who taught him these last eight years had breasts. He snapped out of it too late to stop the ball from deflecting off his fingers and striking a first grader in the eye. Sister Mary Michael Martin, the principal, witnessed Ralphie's spastic move and, after comforting the balling little snot-nose, handed Ralphie a detention slip.

"There, Mr. Licastro," she said. "See if you can hold on to that." His friends gleefully pointed out that he was the only kid in Valley of Tears grammar school history to get detention for making an error in a punch ball game.

Ralphie took a deep breath and shook off the willies. *Not this time,* he thought. *This time, I'll be ready.*

"Chump, chump. No battah, no battah," Ralphie's friend, Joey Bonto, said from his position at third base. A slightly built kid small for his age, Joey suffered from a birth defect that restricted his ability to breathe through his nose. Yet that didn't stop him from playing every game like his next breath depended on winning it.

A sandy-haired seventh grader with buck teeth stepped up to home plate.

"Well, if it ain't Bucky Beaver," said Mario as he curled his lower lip under his front teeth. "Look at me," he said, as he sniffed and pretended to chew on a piece of wood.

"In your mouth," said Buck-Tooth.

"Your momma," said Mario. Buck-Tooth bounced the ball and drew back his fist ready to "punch" it, but grabbed the ball with his other hand at the last second.

"Atee eye, 65te eye," said his teammates. "Wait till you're ready." Ralphie nodded to his friend, William "Doc" Valero at first base, the smartest kid in his eighth grade class.

"Put your hands on your knees," Doc told him. "That way, you'll look like a ball player and act like a ball player." Ralphie always took Doc's advice. He didn't know how that would improve his ball playing, but he liked the pose. It made him feel like he belonged on a baseball card. He gripped his knees even tighter, and planted both feet firmly on the ground.

Buck-Tooth bounced the ball again and this time connected. The ground ball skidded across the asphalt toward Ralphie at second base. An easy play, until Ralphie imagined the ball transforming into a burning meteorite. A scenario unfolded in his head. He had arrived from another planet a short time ago, offering to use his superpowers to protect the town. They laughed at him, made fun of his cape. Told him the tights he wore made him look like someone who forgot to put his pants on before he left the house that morning. "Go back where you came from," they taunted. "Who asked for your help?"

He imagined those same people begging him to stop the deadly incendiary now heading in their direction from consuming the helpless town of East Orange, New Jersey. His cape unfurled behind him like the tail end of a comet about to soar across the sky. He placed his hands on his hips striking a true, man-of-steel pose before springing into action.

But as he stood ready to confront the burning threat, it changed back into a harmless pink ball that shot through his legs allowing Buck-Tooth to round first and make it to second base.

"You stink, "said Mario. "I mean, like how many times I gotta' tell you? Keep your eye on the ball." The comment triggered Ralphie's imagination. In it he could see a baseball with an eye in the middle of it.

"I told you, think like a ball player," said Doc as he walked over to Ralphie and slapped his lead-free bottom. A stick figure with a glove and a baseball for a head popped up in Ralphie's mind.

Ralphie shrugged off their comments as he resumed his hands-on-knees position. The game continued.

His mind wandered as he took his turn at "bat," the ball morphing into the faces of the heathen public school boys giving him the finger as he bounced it up and down. He swung hard at it, but missed. When he bounced the ball a second time, he imagined the drunken church janitor trying to get one of the eighth grade girls to join him for a drink of altar wine. He swung with all his might in an effort to defend her honor, but missed again.

On the third bounce, the eighth grade girl from the previous bounce told him to mind his own business. He lashed out with all his might, wanting to punch her as much as the drunken janitor. But he missed the ball a third time, becoming the first boy in Valley of Tears history to strike out in a punch ball game.

His dubious achievement brought on another round of jibes and insults. But Ralphie took it in stride. He knew his shortcomings when it came to sports. When he played catch with his younger brother, Angelo, and his father at home, he noticed how his hands seemed to act like two" like" poles of a magnet, repelling each other so he couldn't catch any ball his father threw at him. No big deal to Ralphie. He preferred spending time in his room, drawing at the makeshift desk his father made him from two-by-four's and plywood, surrounded by his crayons and construction paper. But he soon realized a game of catch in the back yard meant more to his father than to him. His father couldn't hide the disappointment on his face at Ralphie's performance, a look that faded whenever he turned his attention to playing catch with Angelo.

The game ended early when Buck-Tooth rounded third base and hit the ground, tripping on his pants after they had fallen around his ankles. In his haste to return to class after going to the bathroom earlier, he'd forgotten to fasten his belt buckle. Sister Mary Michael Martin declared the game over as punishment for Buck-Tooth subjecting what Sister called, "the many pairs of our innocent, virgin female eyes," to his offensive Mickey Mouse underwear.

Ralphie joined his friends in front of the windows of the kindergarten class. They watched the teacher, a young, shapely woman, place a box of crayons in each desk. Each time she bent down to accomplish her task, she unknowingly waved her red skirt at them like a matador's cape in front of a bull.

"That is one fine woman," said Mario, his hand lingering on his crotch after a healthy squeeze.

"I wouldn't mind being in kindergarten again," said Joey.

"Go ahead," said Doc. "You're short enough." Joey exhaled a wheeze as he gave Doc the finger.

"We goin' to the movies this week? I liked that 'Bowery Boys' movie we saw last Saturday," said Joey.

"Naw, nothin' good playing," said Mario. "Hey, we're kind a' like a 1959 version of the Bowery Boys."

"Oh, yeah? Which one of us is Slip and which one, Sach?" asked Doc.

"Seein' as Slip is the smart one, that would be me," said Mario. "No offense, Doc. I mean, street smart. And seeing' as Sach is the dumb one…" Mario waved his hand in the air. "…the rest of you can decide that one."

"I think it was more fun blowing up that model battleship after the movie," said Joey.

Ralphie had been trying to follow the conversation. "What movie…what battleship..?" he asked.

"Last week we…." Mario looked at Joey and Doc. "Sorry, Ralphie, I thought you were there."

"Uh…no, I wasn't."

"I know what happened…Chi-Chi…Chi-Chi was supposed to call you," said Mario. Chi-Chi Marino's absence today made him the perfect scapegoat. "We invited you but shit-for-brains Chi-Chi forgot to call you."

"The fat pig probably had a Twinkie or something stuffed in his mouth, so he couldn't talk." Joey coughed as the others laughed.

"You'll be happy to know it was Chi-Chi's battleship we destroyed. We put firecrackers in the smoke stacks, lit them and POW…" Doc raised his hands in the air.

"Blew the whole thing apart," said Joey.

"Man, there were bits of plastic flyin' everywhere," said Mario his hand cupped to his crotch. "You should have been there."

"Yeah," said Ralphie. "Guess I should have been."

The shade of the classroom offered little relief for Ralphie and the other boys from the hot afternoon. Sweat from the exertion of recess soaked their tee shirts making them feel clammy and uncomfortable. To make matters worse Sister Concetta insisted they say the first 10 "Hail Mary" prayers of the rosary on their knees.

"We will be crowning the Blessed Mother in a couple of days," she said as she walked around the room making sure everyone knelt up straight. "I can't think of a better way to show our devotion to her and how loving and caring..." She stopped in front of Mario and screamed. "Mr. Briosch, are you squeezing yourself again?" Ralphie stifled a laugh. Everyone knew the folly of trying to break Mario's habit of squeezing his crotch.

"I'm sorry, Sister," he said as he grabbed his other hand instead.

"I suggest you keep your hands behind your back, if you can't control yourself," said Sister. "Remember, you are in the presence of the Virgin," she said as she pointed to the statue of the Blessed Mother perched on a pedestal mounted on the front wall. As she walked away from him, Mario leaned over to Ralphie.

"Bet I could un-virgin the virgin," he whispered. Ralphie snorted as he tried to hold back a laugh. Sister turned to him.

"Something funny, Mr. Licastro?"

"No, Sister," said Ralphie.

"Fine. Then you can start us on the rosary. Begin with the 'Our Father.' "

Ralphie cleared his throat and opened his mouth to start the prayer, when he caught sight of Mario squeezing his member as he pointed to the statue of the Virgin Mary. Ralphie resorted to a series of short coughs to disguise his muted laughter. He regained his composure.

"Our Father, who's Art in heaven, hallowed—"

"Who's Art?...Who's Art?" Sister pounced on Ralphie. She grabbed his arm and shook him. "Do you think our father in heaven is called 'Art?' Do you?"

"No, Sister...Sister...I think I said 'who art in heaven,' I did." The words vibrated out of Ralphie's mouth as she shook him harder.

"That's not what I heard. I heard, 'Who's Art in heaven...' "She appealed to the rest of the class. "Who else here heard that?" All the girls raised their hands, which didn't count as they instinctively boarded any bandwagon that would contribute to the punishment of a boy, regardless of the circumstances.

"Calling our Lord Art... Art? What kind of a name is that for the Supreme Being?" Sister stopped shaking Ralphie. He stood trembling on his knees, his ears ringing from the shaking she had given him. "Answer me, mister," she insisted.

"It's…short for Arthur?"

Ralphie could barely make out the words as Sister Concetta directed Rita DeBilasco to give him 10 demerits. Rita pulled a marble pad from her desk and gleefully recorded the demerits in a column under his name.

Ralphie tried his best to keep a low profile and pay attention to his teacher for the rest of the afternoon. Sister Concetta stood at the board talking about sentence diagramming and the huge role it would play in their lives. Ralphie's doubts about the importance of diagramming in the long run degraded into boredom. His mind drifted out the window, the ethereal edges of a daydream carrying him along with the clouds in the sky, their varied shapes resembling human figures with fluffy white hair and puffy faces. A voice interrupted his outside musings.

"Sister, Ralphie Licastro is daydreaming again." Ralphie glanced at his teacher, his eyes still dazed from his imaginary wanderings, then toward the voice. Stevie Abadano, the class bully who made Ralphie a frequent target, drilled him with his trademark inane smile. Ralphie's heart raced with a mixture of fear and anxiety every time Stevie picked on him, since the day in first grade when Stevie pushed him on the ground. He laughed at him then and called him a "tar baby, darker than a lump of coal." He harassed Ralphie at every opportunity, smashing his sandwich with his fist at the lunch table and spilling the contents of his desk on the floor. Ralphie wanted to explode at him. But the eruption he sought got stuck in his throat. No one dared challenge the bully.

"That's enough, Mr. Abadano," said Sister Concetta. "I see Mr. Licastro is daydreaming again, I don't need you to remind me." Ralphie avoided Sister's icy stare. "Rita, give Mr. Licastro three demerits." He watched as Rita DeBilasco again pulled out her marble pad from her desk and recorded the demerits. Ten demerits in one week warranted a detention for the offending student. Sister kept her eyes on him as she spoke to Rita. "And how many demerits does our illustrious daydreamer have so far this week?"

"23," she said. The class laughed. Sister raised her hand calling for silence. She walked over to Ralphie.

"Sounds like you beat your record set back in fourth grade. Remember? That was 20 in one week." She folded her arms and walked back to the front of the room. "Mr. Licastro, I have watched you for the last few years do your best to disappoint not only your teachers, but your parents and fellow classmates. I've watched you daydream half your life away, get in trouble with your outrageous antics and the drawings…I won't even start." Ralphie thought back to one he drew of her as a witch, and wished he had depicted her as a devil instead.

"You're in eighth grade now, going to high school, maybe even college, if you ever get serious." She walked up to him. "Stand up and look at me." Sister stood in front of him, her face expressionless, cold. She pushed the disheveled hair back from his face. She tucked a side of his shirt sticking out over his belt back into his trousers. She straightened his tie. Ralphie could feel the eyes of his classmates on him, hear them laughing. In his mind he imagined a drawing he would do when he got home. It would show an ocean, raging, waves crashing on nearby rocks. In the middle of this tempest he would draw a face, only a nose and mouth visible, and arms thrashing in a desperate attempt to keep the body afloat. Sister Concetta's voice jolted him back to the present.

"Now don't you feel ashamed?"

*****

Joe Cappello is most proud of two successes in 2022: *Sell Bots*, his one act play about workplace harassment, published in the Winter 2022 issue of **The Good Life Review**, and *The Secret of the Smiling Rock Man*, his short story, which won first place in the National Federation of Press Women's 2022 Communication contest.

Honorable Mention   **Conor McAnally**

Bullets in the Water

Mike Carson's head snapped up when the brunette in the corner started mewling. Two guys had her pinned against a pinball machine in the corner of the bar, trying to remove her T-shirt. Mike had been bourboning his way through a Rolodex of regrets when the gang of twenty-some things whacked through the double doors half an hour earlier, full of noise and menace. There had been an edge to the air ever since.

"Just show us the damn tattoo," one of them demanded, hauling at the flimsy fabric.

"Stop it, Karter, please." She was getting desperate. The girls in the group looked away in embarrassed silence as the guys began a chant.

"Show it, show it!"

Mike looked around the bar. Everyone acted as if nothing was happening. He stood and walked over. The brunette was blush red and crying, sensing the battle for her dignity would soon be lost.

"OK now," Mike said, "let's take it easy and settle down."

"Get lost," the Karter kid said, looking up at Mike, "and mind your own goddam business."

"Look, some of us are here for a nice, quiet drink. Why don't you knock it off?"

"Do you know who I am?"

"Sure, you're the bully, trying to humiliate this young lady, who clearly doesn't want to show off her tattoo right now."

"You'll stay out of this, if you know what's good for you," Karter said.

"Yeah? Well, no." Mike stepped forward and snapped the kid's wrists from the brunette, turned him sideways and pushed him away. Mike straightened to his full 6' 2" and squared off against the Karter kid, who nodded to Mike's right with a sly smile. Mike turned and caught a brief glimpse of something just before it connected with his head. It seemed a long way to the floor, so it surprised him when it arrived so quickly.

"Oh my god, Jess.." One of the girls.

"Screw him, he shouldn't mess with us." Jess presumably.

"You could have killed him."

Mike started to get up when a pair of tan cowboy boots filled his vision.

"That's enough, leave it, Karter," the Jess voice said.

"No way" one boot connected with Mike's jaw and darkness came.

*****

Mike came to in custody, arms pinned behind his back, handcuffs biting into the flesh. Two uniformed cops hauled him to his feet. They marched him out to a police SUV and eased him into the back seat. He looked to his right at the line of young, taunting faces in the window of Gold Spurs Bar and Grill as Karter and another girl shot him the finger. the brunette was nowhere to be seen. The officers climbed in, and the SUV pulled away.

"Am I arrested?"

"Yessir," said the cop in the passenger seat. "You most definitely are arrested."

"What for?"

"Assault for starters and whatever else comes up."

"Assault? I was hit in the head and kicked in the face."

"We heard. Self-defense, according to the witnesses. Probably best not to say more till we get to reading you your rights at the station."

"I want a lawyer," Mike said.

"I'll bet you do."

They hustled him out of the SUV and marched him through a side door when they got to the station. A sleepy civilian receptionist looked up in surprise.

"Chief here yet?" asked the chubby driver.

"On his way," she said.

They moved him into a gray, institutional interview room, sat him on a metal chair, removed one handcuff and refastened it to a metal table which was bolted to the floor.

"You have the right to remain silent and refuse to answer questions. Anything you say may be used against you in a court of law. You have the right to consult an attorney before speaking to the police and to have an attorney present during questioning now or in the future." The passenger said. Mike now saw he was a Sergeant called Green.

"I would like an attorney present during questioning."

"What attorney?" said the driver whose name tag said Brown. Green and Brown, both white.

Mike was stumped. He didn't have an attorney here.

"John McKinney."

"Honest John," both officers laughed. "OK, we'll see if we can find him. He's not always in his own bed this time at night, if you know what I mean." Brown winked. It didn't suit him.

*****

Honest John McKinney had to stoop low to enter the interview room. Taking off his hat would have spoiled the image. He arrived around 2:30 in the morning. Underneath the Stetson was his usual attire, a gray western suit with black suede front and back yokes. His starched white shirt and longhorn bolo tie completed the image. He was somewhere in his sixties and looked like he could be related to Ray Benson from Asleep at the Wheel. Mike had seen Ray's huge cardboard cutout beside a little restaurant in the Austin airport as he headed toward arrivals just forty-eight hours earlier. *Doing great*, he thought, *only took you two days to get arrested*. Honest John looked him over.

"Chief tells me you're Tom Carson's son."

"That's right."

"I went up against your pappy a time or two. I'd say we came out even in the end, though he'd say he had the edge. Never met you, I don't think."

"No, we've never met."

"So how come you asked for me?"

"I saw your face on that billboard outside town and I don't know any other lawyers here. I've been gone a long time."

Honest John smiled.

"Honest John McKinney for All Your Legal Needs. Nice to see the power of advertising making a return on investment. Well, let's say I agree to represent you."

He pulled out the other metal chair and sat sideways at the table because his knees would not fit under. He took some reading glasses from his inside pocket. They looked small on his head as he opened a brown folder.

"Let's see now."

His finger moved down the page a worrying distance.

"Assault, battery, disturbing the peace, drunk and disorderly, public nuisance, resisting arrest. Someone has been busy."

"This is complete bullshit. They were molesting a young girl, trying to haul her T-shirt off. I went over to help her and got cold cocked for my trouble and then kicked in the face."

"So, you started the fight."

"I pulled the guy's hands off her and pushed him away."

"That's the assault and battery and disturbing the peace. How about the drunk and disorderly? Could you have passed a sobriety test?"

"I wasn't driving."

"Check that box too, then."

"I'm the one who got assaulted."

"By whom?"

"I didn't see who hit me in the head, but I heard the name Jess. The guy who kicked me in the face was called Karter."

"Oh, see now, that's bad. Probably Karter McMillan. We could press charges, kinda like a counter suit, but I wouldn't recommend going up against the McMillans."

"As in Duke McMillan?"

"Yes, you know the McMillans?"

"My brother Andy was best friends with Zane, never heard of a Karter."

"Younger brother, different mother. Anyway, my advice is the same. Best not to go up against the family."

"So, what are my options?"

"These are all just misdemeanors, but you don't want them on your record. Maybe if you were to apologize and be on your merry way back to New York City, they might all just go away. That's where you live, right? According to your driving license."

"I can't go back to New York right now. Unfortunately, I need to be here for a while."

"I see."

Mike wasn't sure if it was the kick in the head or the bourbon that fogged him, but the haze suddenly cleared.

"Wait, a second. They mirandized me, but they haven't charged with anything."

Honest John smiled and closed the folder.

"Right. These are charges they could bring if they want to." He got to his feet. "I'll just go talk to them and get some clarification." He paused at the door. "Just what is a *New York Chronicle* investigative journalist doing in little old Taborville? You here for a story?"

"A story here? Hell no." Although he needed a story — desperately. A big national exclusive might just...

"What then?"

"I'm just here to sell my uncle's house and mind my own business."

"Doesn't sound like you did too good a job of that tonight."

They released Mike an hour later. Charges were not being brought now, but could be filed at a later date. Police Chief Walter E. Gates, according to the nameplate on his office door, issued a warning.

"It would be best if you stayed out of trouble."

"I'm sure my client will be careful." Honest John assured him.

Outside, he offered Mike a ride in his silver Cadillac, but Mike said he needed a walk.

"Where do you want me to send the invoice?"

"1927 North Street."

"You living there?"

"No, but it's where I get mail."

With a tip of his Stetson, Honest John folded himself into luxury and glided away.

Mike walked out of the car park as a cruiser screamed past him, lights on, siren wailing. The officers looked worried.

*****

Conor McAnally is a former print, radio and TV journalist, producer and director who is now a full time writer. *Bullets In The Water* is his first novel. His short story *The Psychiatrist's Window* placed second in Social Consciousness in 2021's SWW contest. http://conormac.com/

Hamblett Cabin
Photo Submitted by Rebecca Larivee

Honorable Mention   **Craig Higgins**

Artichoke Hearts
and
Chicken-Fried Shark

Bay St. Louis, Mississippi, October 1980

Cold autumn air whips across my face when I turn up the beach road. School's out, and my mind's on digging my toes in the sand before heading home. The sidewalk bites into my Chuck Taylor's, making the soreness in my calves worse. Coach put us through our paces yesterday, running the whole wrestling team like dogs in preparation for the December meet.

Trotting quickly, I pass the Home Plate diner. It's the best place for shrimp in town. From the entrance, a buttery aroma smothers the insides of my nostrils.

Two people, a woman and her young son, step through the front door. The little kid stumbles, nearly knocking me over.

An ice cream cone in his hand plops onto the concrete.

Crying, he levels a finger in my direction. "Hey, pineapple-head. You made me drop it."

I hold up my hands in protest. "Did not."

"Did, too!"

His little heel digs into my foot, sending a sting up my leg. "Ow," I say.

Grabbing the tiny vermin's wrist, the woman glares at me. "Would you watch where you're going?"

A grimace crosses my face. "Hey, I'm sorry."

She drags the little boy away, but not before he turns and gives me the finger. "Up yours, pineapple-head!"

Why do people always make cracks about my hair? "Little boy, you need to learn some manners."

The pair ignore me, bumping through the sidewalk traffic, and around a corner.

Shrugging my shoulders, I push through crowds of sidewalk shoppers. Halloween is only a week away, and folks are getting ready for Trick-or-Treat.

In front of a beauty parlor stand a quartet of girls my age dressed in corduroy jumpers and too-tight designer jeans, their feathered haircuts billowing in the breeze like porcupine needles. Transfixed, they stare at a pyramid of cans behind the storefront window. Next to the stack is an ad that reads

Aqua-Net Blow-Out! Three Cans for Five Dollars!

One girl, a freckled redhead with braces, smacks a gum bubble between her lips. "I'm getting me some. Going to dress up like a witch for Halloween this year."

Her friend snickers. "Nadine, you don't need no spray to look like a witch, hon."

The other girls laugh. I brush past them, stopping at the corner before crossing at the light.

A block up, and I shiver underneath the shadows of the twin chapel spires of St. Adolphus, a rich-boys' private school. It's a spooky place, and the shades those towers cast across the road resemble a pair of shark's fins.

At the intersection, snarling traffic blazes past in both directions along the main road, separating me from the beach. I step out and a white pickup plows past a red light, swerving from side to side. Avoiding its onrushing hood, I hop onto the sidewalk.

A bumper sticker sits plastered on the tailgate, a cartoon picture of Johnny Reb. Dressed in a grey uniform, Johnny lies in state beneath a motto which reads: *Save your Confederate money, boys. The South's gonna rise again.*

Just like the little kid, the driver flips me off before zigzagging into the traffic.

A shiver runs through my spine. Nothing like a little brush with death to start the afternoon.

After that near-miss, I cross the road.

In front of me stretches a concrete staircase which descends to chalky sand dotted with plastic bottles and driftwood shards.

A briny stench irritates my nose. I sneeze and almost trip over a maggot-filled dead fish. Avoiding the wretched husk, I stumble down a couple steps until something catches my eye. Fifty yards away, a shiny cabbage-ball-sized object sticks out from the base of a wooden pylon beneath a pier.

It looks valuable. Definitely interesting.

The tide rolls in, scattering driftwood fingers jutting along the wet silt around the object. A couple more rounds like that will wash it back into the bay.

On the steps I hesitate, my breath coming in steam puffs.

Should I grab it?

A raspy whisper growls in my head. *Stupid, stupid, stupid. Who leaves anything nice on the beach?*

Here come the voices. Again.

It's just a dumb piece of junk. Leave that thing alone.

Shut up. Maybe it fell off a rich person's boat. Might be worth a lot of money.

That's stupid.

Is not.

The surf crashes in.

Pain ripples through my stomach.

Well, if you're going to do it, stop being such a wimp and go grab the thing.

I'll grab it when I want.

Stupid, stupid, stupid –

Just shut up, okay?

Bolting down the steps, my canvas high-tops dig ankle-deep into murky sand. Grains of it slip into my socks, irritating my skin. When I reach the pier the tide rolls in, soaking my shoes.

Reaching the pylon, I find the object. Its surface radiates with an iridescent, radish-purple hue. Tapered on one end and covered with overlapping scaled leaves, the body curves on either side like an upturned heart. Tiny, translucent hairs whip the space round a puckered orifice at its exposed apex.

A purple artichoke? Maybe. Except artichokes don't come in that shade.

So, what is it, really? A vegetable? Some kind of sea anemone?

But something about its irregular shape jogs my memory.

The UFO magazines I collect always have articles about stuff like this artichoke. Unexplained finds the government doesn't want people to know about.

Which totally makes it a prize.

Grabbing the thing, I try to yank it from the ground. The leaves' serrated edges rip my hands. "Ow."

I inspect the damage. Red welts sprout around the cuts, itching like a hundred ant bites.

Stupid, stupid, stupid. You'll never get it out like that.

And I won't. Better make a trip to the store.

*****

Smarting from the cuts on my hands, I trot along the main road and up three blocks to a squat building nestled amid a blacktop parking lot.

Jitney Jungle.

The only grocery store in town, on afterschool Fridays its aisles are packed with customers. Matronly housewives pushing stuffed shopping carts strive for supremacy against errant teenagers in search of candy and chips.

The magazine rack tempts me with comics and pro wrestling magazines. But an image of the artichoke stuck in the sand overrides any and all distractions. A list of items I'll need to retrieve it circulates in my head: rubber gloves, trash bags, an aluminum foil roasting pan.

Navigating the crush of bodies and baskets, I locate the gloves and bags on the household goods aisle. But the pan is on another. A screaming little boy clips my thigh on the way to retrieve the last item. This knocks me off course, right in front of a display advertising toaster pastries.

Chocolate Fudge Pop-Tarts. Only $1.99, the sign says.

Searching my wallet, I find a ten. It's just enough to cover everything, the pastries included.

Customers clog the checkout lines. One is for ten items or less, a better fit. I avoid it, pushing through to the last lane. It's the busiest, but I don't care.

Behind the counter, Katie Sue Carson makes the cash register sing.

Four years older than me, Katie Sue is the most beautiful girl in the world. She's thin of build, and kind of tall. Long, chestnut-brown hair falls like rain down her back. Oversized glasses frame sparkling eyes set like sapphires within her round face. Full lips curl into an ever-present smile.

"Mickey Finley," Katie Sue says. "It's so nice to see you."

Time stops.

My tongue thickens into knots.

In my head, I reach across the conveyor belt and pull her to me, us making out like the couple in the Irish soap commercial on TV …

Her brow furrows. "Mickey?"

"Hey kid," somebody says behind my back. "You're holding up traffic."

Whoops.

"Oh, hi," I put the items on the conveyor belt. "How's life in the grocery business?"

"Kind of sucks but it's college money." She scans each item's bar code, then sets it on the counter. "How's your cousin?"

"Tommy? He's alive, I guess."

Big-shouldered, curly-haired Tommy is Uncle John and Aunt Margene's youngest son. He played football in high school and all the girls adored him.

"Alive? I heard he went into the Navy." The register chimes like a pet store parakeet. "Y'all must be so proud of him."

Katie Sue blushes. She used to be one of those adoring girls, which doesn't fit my plans for us at all.

"Yeah, he's pretty cool."

"Well, tell him I said hello. That'll be $9.34."

"Okay." The ten floats out of my wallet.

She stares at my hands while giving me the change. "My word, Mickey. What did you do to yourself?"

I stuff them in my jacket. "Slipped on a rock at the beach."

"We've got some hydrogen peroxide in the breakroom. If you want, I could send somebody –"

"Really, I'm okay."

"You sure?"

"Yeah."

"Okay, well take care now." She smiles like an angel. "Don't run in the traffic."

*****

The artichoke squats in the shifting silt, its lacquered leaves drying out with the receding tide. Cold bites into my knuckles before I put on the gloves. Its mouth puckers, then spits out a puff of dust that smells of rotten eggs.

Grabbing it by the base, I pull the thing upwards.

It lets out a piercing whine, high like a dog whistle.

Rooted in the sand, it doesn't budge until I crouch over it, knees bent. Lifting with my legs, I hoist the artichoke onto the roasting pan. It squirms on the soft aluminum, coughing up a load of plum dust that covers my face.

My nose itches from contact with the murky vapor. I sneeze, then wipe purple soot from my face.

84

The concrete steps stand fifty feet away, a means of escape.

I can leave this, right here. Just forget all about it.

A knot forms in my stomach. *Stupid, stupid, stupid. Stop being such a sissy-baby.*

Ignoring the voices, I push the pan with its burden inside the bag, but the plastic rips in contact with the artichoke's sharp leaves. Doubling up provides enough tensile strength to prevent another gash. Sniffling from the dust in my nose, I toss the gloves onto the sand, then throw the bag over my shoulder. Its squirming contents smack into my back like somebody hit me with a medicine ball. But the pan protects me from the artichoke's thrashing. Grabbing the sack filled with the Pop-Tarts in my other hand, I stare at the top of the steps where the cars pass in silhouette along the road.

Time to go home with my prize.

*****

Aunt Margene and Uncle John's place sits on a quarter-acre lot, a thirty-minute walk from the beach. When I get there, the sun burns orange on the horizon.

I clutch the handle to the kitchen door. A whiff of cooked beef smothers my nostrils, smelling so good it makes my mouth water.

Aunt Margene sits at the table, a telephone receiver nestled between her chin and shoulder. She's about forty-five, plump with greying hair. I find it really easy to talk to her, and consider her one of my few friends, even going back to before I moved in.

"Aunt Margene. I found this cool thing at the beach –"

She glares at me. "Not now, Mickey."

"Sorry."

Brows knitting, she speaks into the phone. "Alright, Isobel. Now, tell me what happened ... really? The officer at the scene said that? What happened to the other guy?"

"Who are you talking to?" I set the bag on the floor.

Aunt Margene holds her hand over the receiver. "Mickey, please. This is serious."

She listens to the person on the other end of the line. I open the box of Pop-Tarts. Ripping the wrapper off one pack yields an aromatic chocolate smell. The pastry slips between my lips, tasting bittersweet.

Tears well in Aunt Margene's eyes. "Oh, Isobel. I'm so sorry to hear about this … yes, I'll miss her, too. We loved that girl. She was like family to us."

The hairs on my ears stand on end. *Who* was like family? What are they talking about?

"Okay … we'll be by the church later. Love you, too. Goodbye." She cradles the receiver on the phone. "Mickey, do you remember the Carson girl? Katie Sue?"

"Um, actually I just saw her like an hour ago."

"That was Miss Isobel, from church." She grabs a tissue and blows her nose. "There's been a terrible accident."

"An accident?"

"Yes. Katie Sue's been –"

"Katie Sue's been what?"

"She's dead."

The pastry falls from my mouth.

My fingers and toes go numb. That loss of sensation travels along my limbs and stops at my heart, deadening my pulse.

Katie Sue, gone. It can't be true.

Aunt Margene cries, "Oh Lord. What's become of this world?"

I wrap her up in my arms and we hug each other tightly.

Outside, the sun slips under the tree line like a hanged man choking on a noose.

*****

Recovering Catholic school boy **Craig E. Higgins** is a fan of sword-and-sorcery and Southern lit. His tales combine teen angst with deep-fried cosmic weirdness. Active in several writers' groups, Higgins is finishing his first novel. The writer and his wife live in Nevada, somewhere between Las Vegas and Area 51.

Honorable Mention   **Vicki Felmlee**

Defiance, West of the River

Dust Devils

July, 1969

Jemmy descended the wide staircase into the living room. The walls gleamed from a fresh coat of paint, the new upholstered furniture gave a welcome feeling. The wide planks of the wood floor had also been refinished, the pleasant odor of lemons and cleaning oil mingled in the air.

She found Helen sitting at the dining room table, waiting for her with a tall glass of iced tea. "Thought you'd be ready for a break," Helen said, pushing it forward as Jemmy sat down.

"It's going to be so good for somebody to be living here again." Jemmy smiled at her old friend. "I want it to be perfect." She curled a bit of hair, now white from age, around her ear.

"And I suppose you want it to be 'perfectly perfect' for that reporter from *Life Magazine*?" Helen's voice was chiding, disapproving.

"Why wouldn't I? That kind of attention will be good for the ranch."

Their nephew had called two days before to say he was bringing a reporter from the national publication. Defiance Mesa, one of the largest ranches in Colorado, had been the subject of many newspaper articles before, local and the Denver papers, but nothing like *Life*.

"What if they ask about the murders?" Helen leaned back, tried to relax. "Reporters always ask about them, usually with that sly, snotty smile hiding a morbid curiosity, trying to draw out some new, gruesome memory."

Jemmy shrugged. "Come on, it's *Life*. Big full-color pictures, a fluffy story. But if they do, I'll bring out those yellowed newspaper articles. Although," she smiled, "you can hardly read them now, it was so long ago."

"And Samson's —" Helen began, but was interrupted with the slamming of the back porch's screen door.

"Mom? Aren't you done cleaning? You've been at this for three days now." Betha walked through the kitchen to join them. She had inherited her long, blond hair from Jemmy and her nose and cheeks were covered by a blanket of freckles, giving her a "little girl" look despite being almost forty years old. "Come outside. The older kids have gone swimming in the lake and we're setting up the badminton net for the little ones." She remained standing but reached for Jemmy's half-full glass of tea.

"I'm almost done. The house is about as ready as it's going to be." "The nursery is so cute. I love the baby ducks and chicks on the wallpaper. And that crib.." Betha kept talking to her aunt as Jemmy stood up and crossed the room to step through the open front door.

Outside, Jemmy breathed in the delicious aroma from dozens of rose bushes planted years before in a hop-scotch manner around a stone path. She took in the blue sky dotted by a few lazy clouds. This vast land. The river's water shining in the distance. The old cottonwood trees lining the road. Cows grazing in the upper fields. She watched as a sudden gust of wind stirred up dirt and a few dried twigs, a dust devil. Circling, circling, rising to a few feet above the ground before just as quickly dying in the air.

That gust of wind, lasting only a few seconds, seemed to taunt her, forcing her to remember the autumn of 1929. That autumn when she was so angry, filled with shame and hatred, wanting people to pay, to suffer, for what they had done to her. That autumn when she was going to leave this place, disappear, never come back.

She almost did.

Almost.

*****

October, 1929

Jemmy Lanson laughed as John O'Brien climbed out of his Chrysler Imperial, struggling with one hand to hold the door open, his other hand to keep his bowler hat on, but failing at both.

"The Devil's let the wind loose today, John," she shouted above the wind.

The hat flew off his head despite his best efforts. "And now my damned hat is loose, too." Running, bent over, he managed to catch the bowler before it crossed the road, and jogged back to the car. "No use wearing it today." He tossed it into the back seat, then joined the women in the driveway. At just over six feet, John was stocky, but well-muscled, with a ready smile and large, brown eyes.

His wife Ottavia was already out of the passenger seat, her long skirt swirling in the wind. She had coiled her brown hair into a tight bun before leaving the house, knowing the wind would be a problem. She wore a knit scarf around her long neck, dark green that matched her eyes.

Jemmy had also thought to capture her own long hair in a loose braid but it still whipped about in the wind, blonde curls threatening to escape. Her face was sunburned, making her startling blue eyes stand out even more. She was a short woman, slender, not even thirty years old – and already a widow. She held on to a small cotton bag with both hands.

Ottavia hugged Jemmy. "Haven't seen much of you these past few days, everything as it should be?"

"No. I'm still going around and around with Uncle Samson about my land," Jemmy said. "I don't know what to think. I need to deliver those final papers to that water board and hopefully get water from the creek before next spring. I gave him the last payment four months ago. Ten years paying him for that little scrap of worthless land." She didn't want to admit her uncle intimidated her. He had a violent temper that was well-known among many in town.

Ottavia put her arm around her, exchanging glances with her husband. "Let John help, he knows how these things work. Being the county's only architect has got to be good for something. He can talk to Samson." At this, John grimaced but didn't say anything. Talking to Samson Black was not on his list of things to do – ever.

Jemmy saw the look on John's face. "The two of you are so busy..."

"Too busy," John agreed, hoping that would end the discussion. It didn't.

"We need to get this done," his wife insisted. Jemmy was more than a neighbor, she was a good friend. "It's been going on much too long. We'll find some time in a few days." She changed the subject to a neutral one. "You've been getting some sun."

"Been trying to fix the gate for the goats but can't seem to get it tight enough. They keep leaning against it." She sighed, then handed the small bag to Ottavia. "I managed to get some cheese made yesterday. Garlic, onion, and herbs. They always sell fast. I'm thinking about upping my price from thirty cents to thirty-five cents. What do you think?"

"You'll have no problem selling them at any price." Ottavia took the bag from her. "You are coming today, for early supper? It's the last Saturday we'll have with the boys for several months. I have venison marinating in the pantry." The boys – twins Davey and Dwaine – were taking the 10-hour train ride to Fort Collins Friday next, starting their second year at the Agriculture College.

Jemmy nodded. "I'll bake some pies today."

They turned to watch Helen Bock coming around the back of her house, juggling several flats of eggs in her arms. She was tall but her long arms were almost no match for the breakable burden she carried. She was dressed in high leather boots and old, stained coveralls. Her black hair whipped around a face that was wide, set with an angular nose and large dark brown eyes. A stranger would call her "handsome" – and that stranger would not know she was one of the largest land owners in these parts, as well as one of the richest women as well. She was only twenty one.

John hurried over to help, taking the top half of the flats from her. "How many dozen do you have?"

"Seven," she told him. "The hens are still laying pretty good now, the nights aren't too cold yet. Next month they'll start to slack off."

The wind picked up. A low and heavy bank of storm clouds gathered to the north.

John secured the egg flats in the back seat, checking his Cartier strap watch. It was just past six thirty in the morning. "Got to get to town, the Mercantile is almost open" he scolded, his voice raised above the wind. "Busy day, busy day."

John and Ottavia returned to their seats, doors slammed, gears shifted. The automobile gave out a loud *"Bang"* with a plume of black smoke from its tail pipe.

Both Jemmy and Helen laughed. "That's going to put John in fine fiddle. He hates that car," Jemmy said. They watched as the big automobile lurched its way down the hard-packed dirt road.

Helen looked about the yard for Jemmy's cocker spaniel. "Where's Dazzle?"

Jemmy pointed to the small black dog, tail wagging, on the porch near the kitchen door. "Smart enough to stay in out of this wind!" Dazzle bounced down and came running at her low whistle. Jemmy scooped the happy little dog up in her arms.

Helen opened the barn's wide door. The loud, high-pitched bleating of two hungry calves immediately greeted them. "Let's get them their breakfast. Then we'll go into my house, it'll be nice and warm. I want you to do a favor for me."

*****

"A friend said he saw several Injuns in the Hunting Grounds last week. Might have been ten or twelve of them. Big powwow like they have sometimes, most likely there're more of them where they're headin'." Samson Black helped himself to a piece of jerky from the counter jar and continued, "I know the Sheriff's going to be watchin' 'em."

Mick Mickleshevsky stood behind his counter, frowning. He placed both hands on the flat surface, his arms rigid. "That'll be a nickel,

Samson," he nodded to the jar. He didn't try to hide his tone. He did not like Samson Black.

Samson dug the coin out of a pocket with grimy hands and tossed it on the countertop . The metal clinked against the wood. "With all those cows still moving down from the high country," he went on, "you can bet there'll be cattle russlin.' Those Injuns in the valley right now ain't no coincidence." Samson was a short man, thin and wiry; his long brown hair was long and bunched together in a pony tail. He was dressed in dirty pants with an equally dirty shirt that might have been light blue at some time. He had a bulbous nose and tiny eyes that were always squinting.

"Hell, it's been what, only six, seven years since that uprising in Utah? Just tell everybody to be on the lookout, they'll be coming back this way, we're sure of it." With that vague warning, he started for the door, pausing on the landing to take a cigarette out of his shirt pocket. He lit it with a safety match struck against the door's frame. A cloud of smoke enveloped his head within seconds. "I'll be over at Mario's, had to drop off a dead pig to him this morning." With that he stepped off of the landing and headed down the road.

Eleanor, Mick's wife, appeared behind him. "What a numbskull." She made a clicking noise with her tongue. "He thinks you're going to spread his gossip? If there's any 'cattle rustlin' going on, my money says Samson's doing it."

She had been sweeping the back aisles, a deliberate and useful way to avoid Samson. Now she slipped on a full-length apron over her slight frame. She gathered her dark red hair in one hand and twisted efficiently twisted into a bun on the top of her head.

Mick reached down to tie the back apron strings for her. He was a tall man, lean, and nearly bald. He still looked younger than his late thirties, perhaps helped by a thin, black moustache. His brown eyes were set wide in a face that featured full lips and a long chin.

"Good ol' Pig Eyes," he chuckled, using the nickname Samson had been given years ago. It was not a complimentary term, and it fit him since he actually did raise pigs. "He always finds a way to make his own trouble, nobody needs to make it for him. Never buys anything from us, just comes in to move his jaw up and down, then I hear he goes to Junction to buy his feed and supplies. Horrible little man, and his brother's a preacher..."

He was interrupted by a loud shuffling noise coming from the back of the store. "That's Darcy," Mick explained to his wife's quizzical look, "getting those sacks of onions for the Potters. I asked him to bring those wooden boxes of canned goods from the deck, put them on the floor, easier for you to get at."

She smiled, appreciating her husband's consideration. "Is he leaving tomorrow?" she asked.

"Far as I know. I think he's impatient to get down to Alamosa before the snows hit but the Potters needed him to get that new ditch in so it'll be ready next spring."

"Potters are going to miss him. And they're not the only ones. I think I'll just mosey on back there and see if he needs some help." Her smile was teasing, even flirty as she headed for the dock.

Mick chuckled at his wife, amused by her play-crush on the young farm hand.

*****

John steered the Chrysler down the smooth, packed road the few miles to the turn off that led to town.

"I'm worried about Jemmy," Ottavia said. She couldn't let go of her concern. "She hasn't been up at the house in more than a week, that's not like her."

John glanced at his wife. "Maybe, well, it's her uh, you know...?" The suggestion was timid, his tone uncomfortable when talking about "women conditions."

"John, women's troubles and moods can't all be put down as a result of our menstruation cycles," she retorted, exasperated at her husband.

He blushed, patted her on the knee. "I understand, I just don't want you to be worried about her. She's coming for supper today? You heard her."

"Yes, maybe I'll get a better read then. She hates her uncle, with good reason. I just wonder if there's something else." She craned her neck to look out the window. "Might get a good storm tonight," she muttered. Around here, seasons were bookended by hot summers and cold winters. Storms carried rain from the south during the summer; snow from the north in the winter.

There was a low but sudden rumble in the sky. Ottavia frowned. Thunder on the left was a bad sign. She didn't mention the old superstition to John, he had little patience for such things.

He gave her a side glance, frowning. "I know you think I can help Jemmy with her uncle, but I don't know anything about water law."

"You can learn?"

"I'm not sure. I'll ask around a bit next time I'm in Junction. But," he perked up, "I can hire somebody to get that goat gate fixed for her. That will be the least I can do."

There was another peel of thunder and the wind picked up.

"Glad we got the cows to auction last week, but we still have to get the field ready for the apple trees," John said. "*And* get the boys on the train to Fort Collins. *And* I've got to deliver those final drawings to the Delta banking committee. Weather allowing, they'll be breaking ground on the new building next month."

"Maybe we should put off the orchard until next Spring?"

John shook his head. "No, I'm obligated to Mick to put that order in. Remember, the field agent said autumn is the best time to plant. The boys and I will get the field cleared Monday and Tuesday, just fifteen trees we're planting after all, not a big area. Then you, me, Jemmy, and Helen can plant the trees when they're here in two weeks."

He down-shifted the Chrysler as he crossed the narrow, one-lane bridge over the Gunnison River. The boards were old wood and rumbled with protest as the car made its way across the long expanse. He approached the intersection to the state highway, a black, oily road running from Montrose to Grand Junction. It had been completed a few years before with great fanfare and celebration, this part of the state at last getting the money for such a project was a very big accomplishment.

The car lurched, threatened to stall as it slowed down. He released the clutch and grimaced as gears ground and the car responded with another loud "Bang" as it shot across the intersection.

"John," his wife chided, "you have to look both ways before crossing."

"Nobody's coming and that road is narrow. Besides, if I slow down too much the damned car shuts off and I'll never get it going again. I hate this damn car." "One day there **are** going to be enough vehicles coming and going, you'll have to mind it and pay attention," she grumbled.

John took a sharp right, and seconds later braked to a sudden stop in front of Mick's Mercantile and Farmer's Supply. This time there wasn't that loud *bang* and John said a silent prayer of thanks especially since there was a wagon with two horses at hitch nearby.

Ottavia read his mind. "Thank the Good Lord you didn't spook the horses."

He leaned over to kiss her cheek. "I thank the Good Lord many, many days, for many, many things," he answered; she knew he meant it.

*****

Vicki Felmlee grew up listening to relatives' stories about life on Colorado farms and ranches, and lived on a ranch as a child. After obtaining her B.S., she was a newspaper and magazine reporter/editor. She is past-president of the National Old Spanish Trail Association, and writes about history at americamoreorless.com.

Honorable Mention   **Roger Floyd**

The Diplomat

In a silversmith's shop you'll find lots of spoons. That's one thing the silversmiths on the planet Anthanos II made plenty of. But as he stood in a silversmith's shop in New Sabean, the capital city of the newly colonized planet of Anthanos II, the spoon the diplomat Marus cradled in his hand wasn't like any he'd seen for many years, and he had a collection of more than four thousand at his home on the planet Pales.

The time factor was 565.003, and Marus had arrived on Anthanos II only the day before to take his yearly relaxation. He regularly visited this planet shortly after the new year's celebration, and the day after his arrival—in a personal ritual from which he never varied—he stopped in at the silversmith's shop.

In his immaculate all-white outfit of shirt, jacket, pants, and black boots, the six foot three inch tall—and slightly portly—Marus always insisted on presenting an image of sophistication and refinement to any world he visited. Well-known and well-liked on many planets in this sector of the galaxy, he took his prominence and reputation seriously, and notable in that care was his appearance. His hair, a nice full head though perhaps a little thin on top, and now in his advanced years almost entirely a striking silver gray, was always groomed, like his clothes, expertly and fastidiously. But his clean, unspoiled look was more than a personal statement—it was a subtle declaration to those around him: "Here I come."

Marus had set his walking stick—he would never call it a cane— on the counter beside the tray of about thirty spoons the silversmith had selected especially for one of his most prestigious customers. Marus browsed the spoons and selected one. The smith placed it in a protective white cloth bag and Marus expressed his thanks and turned to leave. But as he stepped toward the door, he glanced to his left at another display cabinet, smaller, not as well lighted, and set off to the side of the shop. Within that cabinet one particular spoon caught his eye.

"I beg your pardon . . ." Marus pointed to the spoon. "May I see it?"

The smith retrieved the spoon and handed it to Marus. To anyone not acquainted with the fine points of spoon collecting, it might appear as just another spoon. The handle was slightly longer than most, and the tapered oval bowl marginally wider, as though it had been made for a chubby hand to hold and a chunky mouth to feed. But to Marus, two other characteristics of the spoon made it unique to his practiced eye and drew him to it. First, he examined the details of the design and workmanship. A name immediately popped into his mind.

"Saen Bolen. I never thought—"

"I beg your pardon?" The silversmith stood on the other side of the display counter, watching Marus carefully.

"The smith who made this spoon. I recognized his handiwork immediately. He always signs his name in a groove on the back—" Marus flipped the spoon over. "—yes, here it is. I have in my collection a number of his spoons. Over twenty, I believe. But that was many years ago. Might I inquire how you obtained it?"

"Truth be told, I purchased it from a jobber who got it from some planet—I don't remember the name—about four hundred light years away. He asked only four monetary units—"

"The Taanchan Home World." Marus's attention remained on the spoon and he spoke without looking up.

"I beg your pardon?"

"The Taanchan Home World. That's where the smith who made this spoon lives. Saen Bolen. He is Taanchan and his planet is the Taanchan Home World. Oh, I beg your pardon—my apologies. I interrupted you. You were saying . . . ?"

"He asked only four monetary units for it. That's much less than the cost of the silver in it. I rarely take off-world items, but the workmanship is flawless, and he seemed determined to get rid of it."

"I can imagine," Marus mumbled, but almost absentmindedly because he'd turned his attention to the other unusual characteristic of this spoon, the handle.

At the far end of the handle was a set of three circular decorations, arranged in a line down the handle. Each was an engraved representation of a planet Marus had visited, in some cases many years ago. The first was a hot, dry, dusty planet with a toxic atmosphere and daytime temperatures that could exceed 50°C.

Curious, Marus thought. *Why would he engrave* that *on a spoon and send it here?*

The second decoration illustrated a different planet, one with more moderate temperatures and an atmosphere more agreeable to life. Still, the Anthanians knew nothing about either of the planets depicted, or the spoon's planet of origin, so why would the spoon maker engrave these particular planets on what was otherwise an excellent example of his smithing skills? And why would he send it to Anthanos II, more than four hundred light years from the planet on which he lived? Even more curiously, the spoon maker had engraved a small letter over those two planets, a letter in the alphabet of his own language. It would have been an enigmatic sign to an Anthanian, but Marus recognized the letter and understood its significance. Still . . . *why would he depict that planet? And why send it to Anthanos II?* His curiosity escalated and Marus turned to the third planet.

But when he examined the engraving of the third planet, he turned speechless and dumbfounded. He stared long and hard at it, first by naked eye, then through a small magnifier he borrowed from the silversmith. He recognized immediately the two geologic formations depicted in the engraving—formations that told him he was looking at Anthanos II, the planet on which he now stood and visited yearly. He glanced up at the silversmith, his bewilderment multiplying.

"I find myself at a loss . . . I shall purchase this spoon. Thank you for your time."

The silversmith placed the spoon in a second bag and Marus left the shop. But the spoon and the tantalizing mystery of its engravings continued to swirl through his mind as he made his way down the street.

The silversmith's shop stood near the far end of a three-block-long dead-end street in the burgeoning city of New Sabean. Situated along this narrow street, named Artist's Way, a short spur off the main downtown business district, were the artist studios and galleries, the glass blowers and silicoartisans, the sculptors and metal workers, as well as a few microbreweries, cafés, and intimate clubs. As Marus walked back down the street and into the seasoned vapors that came from one of the nearby food vendors, he heard the seller advertising his particular concoction and he inhaled the aroma that came through the shop's open door. "Get yer tacha right here, folks, best tacha on the planet, best tacha above zero level."

Marus looked up at the sign over the door. In bold letters it read: "Delagorian Tacha and Kielkus, Hot and Ready to Go."

Ah, yes, kielkus, the one Anthanian delicacy that instantly recommends itself. Perhaps I should stop in and order a serving. It is, after all, close to time for the second meal of the day.

Then, briefly and without understanding why, his eyes drifted down to the lower part of the sign. It read, in a smaller font than the lettering above, "L. Delagorian and Son, Proprietors." His eyes dallied on the word "Son," and in one of those exceptional instances that happens to almost everyone but which can never be fully explained, and results in a *nouveau* recognition of something seen many times before, he'd solved the riddle of the spoon and everything fell into place like the pieces of a puzzle. He took a deep breath and blurted out to the street around him.

"Of course! It's the *son*. It has to be the son—the old man is certainly dead by now . . . oh, my God." He pulled the spoon from his pocket and stared at it. The significance of the three planets and of the two letters gelled in his brain. His heart pounded, his head spun, and he leaned against the doorframe of the shop to steady himself.

One passerby stopped, concern in his voice. "You okay, mister?"

Marus nodded but said nothing.

An unknown, nebulous voice came from inside the shop. "Can I get you a glass of water? Or jell? Kell?"

"Thank you, no. Your generosity is gratifying but I must be on my way." Marus left the doorway and continued down the street, unsteadily at first and now using his walking stick more than he had in many days. He returned to the Aldon Hotel, a mere five city blocks away where he stayed during these visits, and remained in his room for the entire night. He paced the floor for many hours, ate very little for the third meal, and slept restlessly that night. Early the next day he made an urgent appointment to visit the President of the Anthanian Assembly, an old friend named Tina Leda whom he first met on the original planet of the Anthanian people, Anthanos I, in her office in Assembly Hall.

He knew what he had to tell her. But he dreaded to have to say it.

*****

Roger Floyd is a retired PhD medical researcher who is now committed to writing science fiction and literary short stories full time. He has completed a trilogy of science fiction novels which are in various stages of preparation for self-publication. He also writes a blog about science, writing, and the environment at rogerfloyd.wordpress.com

Honorable Mention   **Jodi Lea Stewart**

Midnight at the Bus Station

1958

I didn't drown in the South China Sea holding Babe's rooster in the air, but almost. A year later, Pinkie and I were chased by cutthroat thugs down a slum street in Los Angeles. My choice of a profession has tossed me into the epicenter of every human endeavor and emotion for the past ten years. I've been praised, cursed, hugged, stomped, chased, and flung through the air. I've danced on tables, bribed hotel personnel, flirted with criminals, and played daredevil with death more times than I care to admit. Why, then, should I find myself so distraught after being pushed from an idling car and having a shoe flung in my face?

I'm working on the answer to that, but I think it's that my previous experiences were expected, embraced, and certainly not personal. To have a presumed friend and colleague turn on me as savagely as a rabid dog this evening seems to have triggered a certain psychological shockwave most likely linked to my, let me say... less-than-perfect childhood.

Little more than a half hour ago, I sat splattered on my derriere in a cold alleyway, broadsided by a man I had respected, a person I have been on assignment with and whom I spent a wonderful three hours with this very night at a company *fête* at the Bangor House reception hall. The remembrance of it starts my hands shaking, and I know what to do about that.

ROSE Recovery number two is the protocol we are trained to follow after any episode following danger.

Deep, slow breaths. Concentrate on your surroundings.

I take in a quick draft of air and blow it out even quicker, then long, slow breaths as I sit expressionless on a plastic chair placed solitarily against the wall. My nylon-stockinged feet are resting on top of what's left of my open-toed high heels. Judging from the stinging in my toes, I believe they were close to frostbite by the time I entered this warm building.

My surroundings? A small, rustic bus station in a four-story brick building in downtown Bangor. I case the room slowly, letting all five of my senses take over. A small huddle of hollow-eyed street people sitting on the floor are excitedly comparing their goods from a day in the streets. My quick perusal shows necks of whisky bottles jutting from tattered cloth bags, half-eaten foods wrapped in crinkled foil, most likely rummaged from restaurant trashcans, and yards of dirty yarn masquerading as skull caps and scarves. How those poor souls avoid freezing to death in this cold-winter city, I do not know.

A station security guard emerges from a door and flushes them outside. He imperiously holds the door open as the mismatched crew marches outside like naughty children. When the last one is through the door, he steps partially outside and peers into the night sky. Tumbling ice crystals shine as nocturnal jewels in the light escaping from the doorway—cotton-wrapped bullets pelting the snow and forming a crust of ice over the streets and sidewalks.

The guard shakes his head and beckons the group back inside, lecturing them with extended finger to stay put and not bother, that is, beg from, anyone in the station. The relief on their blotchy, weathered faces matches his mock austerity.

Flattened garland scotch taped across the ticket windows and a hand-painted *X-mas Greetings!* On the outside doors show a brave attempt to bring holiday spirit into the nearly deserted station. The cream-colored walls sport a long metal cutout of a loping greyhound. Crinkled posters thumbtacked to the walls depict buses traveling on highways passing through redwood forests and alongside sparkly seashores.

I'm calming down. I settle back a few more inches in the chair and continue my study of the room. A young couple sits tight-lipped and straight on the end of a Naugahyde-covered sofa on the opposite side of the room. She is dressed simply in saddle shoes with thick knee-high stockings, a plain shift too thin for winter, and a sweater stretched crooked by a hundred washings. Her coat is draped over the back of the bench, and a modestly wrapped Christmas box is on her lap. Judging from her expression and straight neck, along with the man's restless shuffling and terse glances in her direction, I know they're in the middle of a quarrel.

A fleshy man in a cheap wrinkled suit and loosened tie, who only minutes ago exuded bored resignation and nervous hand clasping, pulls out a white handkerchief and swabs it across his forehead. He isn't all right; anyone can see that. Everything about him, especially his frayed briefcase and out-of-season Panama hat, screams *weary salesman.* In my peripheral vision, I covertly watch him fumble with the folded newspaper on the bench beside him. He works at it until part of a page rips off, then uses it to vigorously fan his face. He exudes a loud sigh, more like a grunt, and, between his spread legs, drops his face toward the tiled floor. His hat falls off, but he doesn't seem to care.

Lord to goodness, is he about to have a heart attack?

Feeling my stare, he glances at me. The lines on his face bear a striking resemblance to a Bristol-paper charcoal etching of an old man I saw in the Louvre Museum in Paris a few years ago. What lot in life has this man traveling by bus in such obvious disappointment and scruffy shoes? Perhaps he was hired to sell French copper cookware to the shantytown wives? That kind of frustration could induce the ruination of anyone.

It hits me with a peculiar, half-jaunty air that I, CeeCee Jones, fit in well with this midnight-at-the-bus-station crowd with my disheveled hair and blood-caked lower lip. I'm a mess right now, and I find that rather memorable. At least it covers up the expensiveness of my clothes—clothes I wore to our celebration tonight. I re-cinch my street-length camel coat, dirty spots and all, and dab my raw lip with a handkerchief. No fresh blood.

My feet are swelling. Shoving my toes back into the narrow strip of see-through plastic across the toe box isn't going to be possible now. Really? I'll have to walk across the room to the ticket area in bare-footed hosiery with more runs humming up and down my legs by the second? A warm flush invades my face as I study the unattractive hole on the left-foot stocking. The hole was made by a bolt I snagged on earlier.

Face burning, I ponder… can I be more of a dichotomy?

I'll dive into a waterway with alligators if I have to, though I did that only once, or tenderly coerce a ship captain with promises I'll never keep in order to distract him, but going barefoot in public with disgraceful hosiery insults my southern roots and pushes me to the edge of vulnerability—an emotion I refuse to entertain.

I sigh abjectly and start across the room. I feel the salesman's crimson-rimmed eyes follow me as I pass him on the way to the ticket counter. I admit that one of my objectives is putting distance between us before he collapses. I simply cannot get involved. Haven't I been through enough tonight? Still, I feel the old twinges of guilt.

Guilt was my constant companion for a good portion of my younger life and one of the strongest catalysts to my seeking the life I now live. I don't regret my history with it. It has proven to be a good and gracious commodity… gracious for me, and good for the ones I *replant,* as Harry Wáng loves to label our processes.

As a matter of fact, my rushing to answer the ever-present siren of distress that only certain people allow themselves to hear is how I met my two favorite *assignments,* Pinkie and Babe.

*****

Jodi Lea Stewart is a fiction author who writes about the triumph of the human spirit through overcoming adversity. Her lifetime friendship with an eclectic mix of all races, cowpunchers, country folks, intellectuals, as well as the southern *gentry*, inspires Jodi to write historical and contemporary novels set in the South, the Southwest, and beyond.

Section Three

Book Review

There is an art to reviewing other's works. This year SWW added a category for Book Reviews.

The entrant could select any book (not your own) and review it in 750 words or less. Must have the Book's Title and Author in the top left corner, but the review itself needed a title.

Review should include what the book is about, their analysis of the book, and where to find it. Include a photo of the front cover for extra points.

Because there were few entries, only one prize was awarded in this category.

First Place   **Roger Floyd**

Santa Fe and the Atomic Bomb

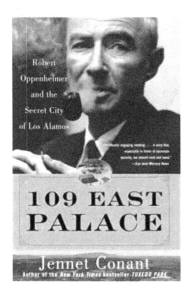

A Book Review of

109 East Palace,
by Jennet Conant,

Simon and Schuster Paperbacks, 2005.

I've read several books about the building of the atomic bombs in Los Alamos, New Mexico, but Conant's book is the first to relate, in her words, the "very personal stories of the project's key personnel." The book goes beyond a description of the building of the bombs, covered adequately in those other works, and introduces us to characters not usually portrayed.

Here we meet Dorothy McKibbin, hired in the lobby of the La Fonda Hotel in Santa Fe, in March, 1943, to run the Santa Fe office of what she was told was a project of "great importance and urgency." Other books on this subject have downplayed Dorothy's role (in some cases barely mentioning her), but Conant brings her to center stage to witness the building of the bomb through her eyes. Dorothy even became known to friends and associates as the "Atomic Lady," though she was never really privy to the details of the work in Los Alamos (affectionately referred to as the "Hill").

The office was at 109 East Palace Avenue in Santa Fe, just a few steps off the Plaza. Though that put it near the center of the city, it was selected largely because it was relatively inconspicuous, set back from the street and guarded by a heavy wrought-iron gate at the door. But McKibbin, the "gatekeeper" to Los Alamos, received many visitors through that office over the years, both well-known and unknown, and dutifully wrote out pass after pass for those visitors—perhaps hundreds of passes in the three years when the work on the Hill was still top secret—so they could travel up the long, winding, unpaved road to Los Alamos and be granted entrance.

The pass was solid gold; it got you in. But Dorothy always had permission from Oppenheimer's office to issue a pass in the first place, and in those years she wrote out only one pass without prior authorization, to Colonel Paul W. Tibbets, the Army Air Corps pilot who had been selected to command the B-29 that would drop the first atomic bomb on Japan.

In 1936, Dorothy built a traditional adobe-style home in Santa Fe on the Old Santa Fe Trail which became an informal meeting place for the Hill's workers. With her distinctive yellow roses blooming in the courtyard, important conferences with out-of-town guests were occasionally held there, even weddings between workers from the Hill.

We also meet, in a somewhat more personal touch than other books, and through Conant's vivid storytelling, many of the key personnel who worked on the hill. Oppenheimer is of course the leading figure here, and Conant goes into detail about his early life and selection to head the project. His wife Kitty was a somewhat more enigmatic person, much more withdrawn than "Oppie" himself, and participated little in the social life on the Hill. She could be charming to some, but to others she was cold and distant, and was even described as "impossible" by one other wife.

Life on the Hill, into which Conant delves in some detail, was far from strictly research and development of the bomb. (Oppenheimer insisted it be called the "gadget" for security reasons.) Hiking in the canyons around the Hill in the summer, and skiing in the wintertime were common sports for the scientists and their families. Neils Bohr was quite a good skier and put younger men to shame by his energetic attack on the slopes.

Family life takes a front seat in the book, too, with Conant going into much of the trials and tribulations of families trying to set up housekeeping on the Hill in what one person described as a "Barnum and Bailey world." We meet also General Leslie Groves, the overall head of the Manhattan Project, but more as a person than as a demanding General used to giving orders.

Dorothy and Oppenheimer stayed in touch for several years after the war, especially during the fervid anti-communistic crusade in the 1950's when Oppenheimer, who had joined the Communist Party in the 30's, was designated—against all logic and reason—a national security threat. Dorothy supported him fully.

I highly recommend Conant's book for its personal touch to what is frequently a controversial subject. More than any other book I've read about Los Alamos and its place in history, this book opens it up in a much more humanistic way. I found my copy at Barnes and Noble, and it's available on Amazon and Thriftbooks.

*****

Roger Floyd is a retired PhD medical researcher who is now committed to writing science fiction and literary short stories full time. He has completed a trilogy of science fiction novels which are in various stages of preparation for self-publication. He also writes a blog about science, writing, and the environment at rogerfloyd.wordpress.com.

Section Four

Elevator Pitch

Here is something a lot of authors don't realize they will need in the world of book marketing. An elevator pitch summarizes a book or movie script - condenses it to a few well chosen words designed to intrigue an agent or publisher quickly.

If you find yourself in an elevator standing next to a publisher, agent, or movie producer and you want to catch their interest you've got to do it quick – before the elevator door opens and they leave.

The Elevator Pitch category is one of three which was thrown open to the entire SWW membership. The votes came out equal on the top two entries, so it was decided that we would give both first place awards. On the next three pages you will see story ideas the membership deemed most interesting.

First Place   **Ed Johnson**

Santiago's Prayer

A dying young man, desperate to give his life meaning, returns to his native mountain village, where he poses as a priest. But his ruse is complicated by the anticipation of war, an atheist who carves saints, a self-righteous woman who's suspicious of him, the birth of an infant out of wedlock, and a weeping statue.

*****

Ed Johnson – No Bio Received

First Place   **Chris Allen**

The Harmonic Chronicles

In a universe where music from Earth acts as a narcotic for alien species, a newly trained female protector from a distant planet is sent to save a young, gifted Irish composer from abduction and exploitation.

*****

Chris Allen, a retired archaeologist, started writing short stories in 2014. Since then, she has won awards for storytelling and editing. Her latest book, *Alchemy's Reach*, co-authored, will be published in 2023 in paperback, e-book, and as an audiobook. She resides in Corrales, NM, with her husband and a menagerie of sheep, goats, horses, and dogs.

Third Place   **William Fisher**

The Price of the Sky

A young aviator turned reluctant bootlegger and bank robber spends his life seeking redemption, clemency, and romance with the unlikely and unexpected help of a politically connected woman. Based on real people and true events gathered from newspaper accounts, official documents, and personal papers. The story is set in Texas and Indiana between 1926 and 1940.

*****

Bill Fisher is a retired Air Force officer and community planner. His first novel, *Cruel Road*, was a 2021 finalist in the New Mexico/Arizona Book Awards for historical fiction and first book. His second book, *The Price of the Sky*, is a true crime historical novel scheduled for publication in 2022.

Section Five

Limericks

Who can resist a good limerick? A poem in the celtic style with a fun twist. A limerick is a five-line poem that consists of a single stanza, an AABBA rhyme scheme, and whose subject is a short, pithy tale or description.

This is another category in which the full membership of SouthWest Writers was allowed to review and cast votes for the winners.

First Place   **Chris Allen**

Words

There once was a woman named Myrtle

Whose prowess with words was quite fertile,

But she got in a bind,

And shattered her mind,

While playing the new game called Wordle.

*****

Christina Allen's latest book, *Alchemy's Reach*, co-authored, will be published in 2023 in paperback, e-book, and as an audiobook. She is a member of the Corrales Writing Group. For more information on Chris and her co-harts you can access their facebook page under the name WritersInCorrales.

Second Place   **Roscoe Champion**

Teen Diagnosis

Her room resembles a wreck to me;

Requests are met with, "Oh, Heck!" to me.

It's medically clear

This growth on her ear

Requires a quick telephectomy.

*****

Roscoe Champion's writings include two volumes of memoirs and 6 books of poetry: *Life in the Watermelon Works* (about people at Sandia Labs), *Flakes of Time, Wandering and Wondering, & Vignettes. And Then* . . . shares memories and healing after his wife died. A delightfully illustrated children's book, *Chrys Caterpillar's Dream.*

Third Place   **Roscoe Champion**

Old Pro Politico

A true politician we know

Spouts spellbinding speeches that glow

With pure obfuscation

And great fascination

With his shining altar: Ego!

*****

Roscoe Champion also wrote this delightful stab at politicians. His poetry and children's books are currently available on Amazon.

Section Six

Haiku

Haiku is an untitled, short verse (often three-lined) that reflects nature and has a surprise last line, called the "ah-ha" of the verse. It is NOT a three-line poem. Without that last surprise line, that twists the reader to a different, often deeper, thought, it is not a haiku.

First Place   **Dodici Azpadu**

Snow dust on the grass

kissing autumn good-bye

weep into winter.

*****

Dodici Azpadu is an American-born Sicilian Arab. Her novels have been nominated for a Lammy, A New Mexico Book Award, and a Golden Crown Literary Award. Her most recent novel is *Portrait Beyond the Frame,* available on Amazon.

Second Place   **Ed Lehner**

Storms pass by unknown

but for dark clouds with strong winds.

Sad salt tears not shed.

*****

Retired professor, **Ed Lehner,** is a luthier, amateur musician, and enjoys writing poetry and fiction. He has written two novels and most recently published an anthology of short stories, ***Grandpa's Horse and Other Tales.*** You'll find more at his website, elehner.com. He hangs out with his wife, Julie, and their cat, Emma, in Southwest Colorado.

Third Place   **Rebecca Dakota**

---

lockdown privilege

a currency of COVID:

new jigsaw puzzle

*****

Rebecca Jo Dakota writes for joy. A longtime resident of Albuquerque, she loves New Mexico skies, grows poppies and peas, cultivates friendships, wins blue ribbons at the state fair pie contest, and shepherds a web site, PiePals.com. She agrees, "Some words end silences. Some words start them."

Honorable Mention   **Wendy Brown**

Delicate blossoms

Cling to bony withered vines

Memories of spring!

*****

Wendy Brown is a (mostly) retired wildlife biologist who spent many years as a field researcher studying birds. She has always written poetry for pleasure, and now has the time to work at it more seriously. Her muse and inspiration is Nature. She especially admires the works of Mary Oliver, Wendell Berry, and Rilke, and Tagore.

Honorable Mention   **Rebecca Dakota**

waiting underground

fertile bulb sits in the dark

wondering what next

*****

Rebecca Jo Dakota writes for joy. A longtime resident of Albuquerque, she loves New Mexico skies, grows poppies and peas, cultivates friendships, wins blue ribbons at the state fair pie contest, and shepherds a web site, PiePals.com. She agrees, "Some words end silences. Some words start them."

Section Seven

Poetry – Free Verse

Perennially our most popular poetry category, Free Verse is simply that – it allows the poet the options of word placement on a page, rhyme, or no rhyme, and optional punctuation and capitalization.

This year we did not specify any topics for our free verse entrants which allows them to enter whatever strikes their fancy. The sheer number of excellent entries made this a difficult category to judge!

First Place   **Kathleen Holmes**

Ode to a Dead Poet

The obituary said you died of

light

    verse.

Ashes from your poems

    will be tossed

    into the wind at

    Two—

followed by a gathering

    on the sidewalk

    to nowhere

    —there will be food.

*****

Kathleen Holmes is a resident of Aztec, NM. She has written feature articles for *The Anvil's Ring* – a magazine for the Artist Blacksmith Association of North America, and short stories in *The New Settler Interview*. In 2021 *A New Mexico Love Story* appeared in the SWW anthology: *Ramblings & Reflections*.

Second Place   **Wendy Brown**

Facing Cancer At the Foot of Ladron Mountain

I pause in the shadow of Ladron Mountain,
which rises, improbably
four thousand feet of ripsawed rocks above the desert.
Standing alone, implacably,
this last defiant warrior
surrounded by a battered field of desolation.

I ask the mountain for courage.
I ask for strength and stamina.
I ask for the grace to face what I must.
But I do not ask for mercy
for I know it cannot be given.

Suddenly
Black arrows fly from behind the rocks.
I hear the swift of their wings
Before I see them inked against the blue.

Five ravens.

They kettle in the wind above me
sailing south, one by one.

The first, tiptoes on the lightest of wings
merrily, and bubbling with the laughter
that only children and ravens possess.
She carries my childhood.

The second, tumbles and dives through air,
reckless, vibrant, beautiful, immortal.
An arrogant acrobat, shouting with extravagant strength.
She carries my youth.

The third flies straight and true,
her voice is a gentle force.
Bearing the burdens of her tribe,
She carries my adulthood.

The fourth flies more slowly, croaking,
then voices a clarion bell, that quiets the others.
Ringing out the gorgeous cruelty of this world.
She is an elder, like me.

The fifth lingers above me, silently
carrying my death.
I watch her for the longest time
But I cannot see where she lands.

*****

Wendy Brown is a (mostly) retired wildlife biologist who spent many years as a field researcher studying birds. She has always written poetry for pleasure, and now has the time to work at it more seriously. Her muse and inspiration is Nature. She especially admires the works of Mary Oliver, Wendell Berry, and Rilke, and Tagore

Third Place   **Victoria Holmsten**

Produce Far Aisle

"Do that somewhere else,"
   said the prune lipped
        banana nosed
        apricot eared
        tomato headed high school librarian
when she caught me lingering over Brave New World

So many places to stop
        squeeze the covers
           sniff the ends
      look for brown spots
  cobwebs and signs of spoilage
Delicious and ripe fruits
So close to my nose and near sighted eyes

It was her mission to keep me away from tantalizing words
        revolutionary black marks on onion white pages
        and artichokian abstractions

I plucked the pages, grape by grape, illegally
        and popped them into my mouth
        hiding behind the stacks of fresh and purple prose

When she turned to restack the encyclopedia display
        I dashed out the back door
        Dickinson and Twain in hand
        dropping strawberry stems as I fled

*****

Vicki Holmsten taught writing, sixth grade through graduate school, mostly in New Mexico. Her short stories, essays, and poetry have won awards in recent years. She is looking to publish her first novel, *Altitude Sickness, A Love Story.* She lives in Farmington, New Mexico.

Honorable Mention   **Alan Bern**

In memory of my Milton teacher, John

in every season you

wrote on the hill

high above campus

in the echoey dark

Café Espresso

now a perky Real

Estate office

everyworkday then

after your wild lectures

with spittled lips

and fingers pointing

in every direction

you wrote by hand

your countless strict-

structured poems

over stillwarm

tea with foamed milk

cooling in a

dull-metal pitcher

perfectly small

and constantly re-

filled by a waiter

smiling in a

starched white shirt

*****

Retired children's librarian **Alan Bern** has published three books of poetry: the most recent is *greater distance, Lines & Faces* 2015. He has won awards for his poems and stories and is an exhibited/published photographer. Alan performs with dancer Lucinda Weaver as *PACES. Lines & Faces,* his press with artist/printer Robert Woods, linesandfaces.com.

Honorable Mention   **Matt Nyman**

A Different Christmas Tree

We got a different tree this year.
Eschewing the common
Douglas fir, Blue spruce or Scotch pine,
we chose a native redwood:
            A narrow soldier-like profile.
            Thin green branches.
            A sturdy trunk.
It's a bit of a nasty tree, actually,
plucking at us with unforgiving needles,
leaving a nasty rash.

This evening the January rain patters our roof.
I imagine the tree hears this symphony of moisture
and even attempts to stretch dormant limbs to the sky.
Maybe the tree remembers a time
with rain everywhere descending, and days she gathered
Earth, Sun and Air to participate in
the sustaining cycles that drive this world.
But not today –
Not even yesterday -
Or a week of yesterdays –
No chance of reaching promised grandeur
and purpose designed within her DNA.

Now it's time for the ornaments to be removed,
loaded into worn cardboard crates,
lights wound around plastic spools.
And tomorrow I will wait with the tree at the roadside
for the great blue truck that will bear her
to the gentle chipper.

*****

Matt Nyman hails from Corvallis, Oregon. He is a geologist, educator and education researcher and recently has dedicated more time to his study of Buddhism, observing the world and writing poetry. This is his second poem that has been recognized by Southwest Writers.

Honorable Mention   **Arlene Hoyt-Schulze**

Skipping Stones

My heart skips across water
once, twice…five times…
skipping beats, splash!
Falling riotously
'tween rocks wet and slippery
as sunlight dances chartreuse
off leaves before embarking
on the journey into dusk.

Bolder sounds the rushing makes,
sneaking into smaller coves
where tiny fish swim in pools
clear with stiller water.
Water's boulder skipping sound
dashes over rocks, coursing
loud and low, soft and high
skipping...like a rock over water.

My heart slides into the river
after a long day's climb over
mountain and through forest,
refreshed in the cool rushing.
Silver strands of water shining
in the hot afternoon sun.
My heart runs down river
dancing in liquid silver.

To the sound of cool breezes
softly blowing tiny fronds
while moss clings to wet rocks,
water gently christens my heart.
The river waits
to baptize others,
ever singing the calming song;
as life's endless flowing

invites my heart
to the river's singing
alive in sempiternal song.
I wait hoping to glimpse what life
the river sings to its side.
The wind's accompanying
melody hastens them
ever calling.

This enduring song fills my mind,
all else is silenced.
At first as one big rushing sound;
carefully I listen
as smaller melodies reveal
life's infinite choruses...

my heart skips...

*****

Author Biographical information unavailable

Flyers
Submitted by Jeffrey Otis

Section Eight

Prose - Flying

This year's contest had four categories for prose stories. The first must have some connection with flying – though we leave it to the author to determine if the flight is in an aircraft, about birds, or possibly flights of fancy.

Prose stories were judged according to standard story arcs and how much of the story is related to the category (i.e., a story where a mountain is mentioned once: "I once saw Mount Fuji" but has no other relationship to the category, will be scored lower than one where mountains are integral to the story). Judges looked for writing that emphasizes creative and intelligent use of the English language to create mood and craft an effective story line.

First Place   **James Tritten**

One Way Flight to Shakin

"Gremlin, this is Wild Stallion three two, ten minutes out." Alex put the ten-minute paradrop checklist back into the map case on his right.

A female voice spoke to the crew over the radio. "Roger Wild Stallion three two, radar contact. Weather at Romeo reported ten thousand broken, winds from the north variable five to ten knots. You're cleared in hot. Beware low altitude rotary traffic to the south and east of Romeo." *Probably an Air Force controller.*

Lieutenant Commander Ron Sequera, in the pilot's left seat, reduced power on the turboprops and descended the Navy fixed-wing airplane. "Alex, I want to get these guys as close as possible to Fire Base Lilley."

"Roger, sir." Alex looked out and saw the moon and stars disappear as the twin-engine stubby Grumman C-2 Greyhound cargo aircraft slipped into the opaque clouds above Paktika Province, Afghanistan.

"Alex, turn off the external lights."

"Roger." *No sense in making it even harder to fly in the soup.*

Commander Sequera asked, "Aft, this is Flight, confirm ready."

Aft, in this case, Petty Officer First Class Charlie Donovan, the enlisted loadmaster, responded with a crisp, "Aye, aye, sir, ready."

Damn, I'm supposed to manage all the communications. Boss needs to concentrate. Flying through the clouds with no visual reference points, Commander Sequera would be relying on instruments at the same time he was configuring the aircraft to execute the mission. It was Alex's first night static line drop.

As co-pilot, he was there to manage the easy stuff, function as safety, and back up the pilot – just in case. *This'll be like we briefed on the ship. Fly in high, drop down at the last minute. Team exits one, two, three. We climb up and head back. It'll all be over in fifteen minutes.*

The primary flight displays showed Commander Sequera had steadied his run-in heading three six zero degrees, due north, at one thousand feet above ground level. They were now below a broken layer of clouds with diffuse moonlight brightening the cabin. The crew executed the three-minute paradrop checklist. Two-thirds flaps were set, power adjusted, and indicated airspeed slowed to one hundred knots. The angle of attack indicator (AOA) read twenty-two units – nose high in a landing attitude.

The old man can really fly this bird in slow flight. The boss had done more than a few of these drops and had taken Alex C'Debaca, a Lieutenant Junior Grade and the detachment nugget with some five hundred forty hours, under his wing.

The pilot reduced power again and held the AOA steady – the vertical speed indicator (VSI) registering a descent. Sequera leveled off at eight hundred feet AGL. Alex set the radar altimeter to provide a verbal "altitude, altitude" warning if they dipped below this level. He glanced outside and could barely make out dark mountains to the west, and Pakistan lay somewhere in the darkness to the east.

"Aft, warn the team I've set two-thirds flaps, and I'll be flying a bit nose up."

"Flight, this is Aft, roger."

"Sir, interrogative two-thirds flaps." *NATOPS recommends one-third flaps for a static line drop.*

"Affirmative, two-thirds flaps. The drop zone is small. I want to get as slow as I can."

"Roger." *Turbulence in the cargo compartment will be a problem.*

They had picked up a SEAL Team on their aircraft carrier not too far offshore in the Arabian Sea. They were taking them deep in-country to support Army Special Forces near the village of Shakin. The SEALS were to protect the eastern flank of a cross-border incursion into Angoor Ada, Pakistan. One of those missions that would never be written about in history books – unless something went wrong.

They completed the three-minute paradrop checklist, and Donovan opened the ramp. Millions of people had watched James Bond and other fictional heroes on the silver screen drop out of the back end of

148

Air Force cargo planes at high altitudes. Today troops went through gaping ramps at the rear of the fuselage. They lowered horizontally, making an exit safer than in the old days of World War II when many parachutists went out through the side of the fuselage.

Frosty night air swirled inside the aft compartment as the Navy SEALS readied for extraction at eight hundred feet.

Commander Sequera spoke into his microphone. "Gremlin, this is Wild Stallion three two, three minutes out."

Should have been faster and made the call myself.

"Roger Wild Stallion three two, cleared in."

"Sorry, sir. I'll get the next one."

The terrified voice from Donovan broke into their practiced routine. "Flight, Aft, we lost one of the SEALs out the back."

"Aft, Flight, you see a chute?" Commander Sequera, the pilot in the left seat, did the talking.

"Negative."

"What happened?"

"Clip failed…"

"Never mind." The pilot switched to his radio. "Gremlin, mark our spot fifteen seconds ago. One of the team got sucked out."

"Roger Wild Stallion three two. You want to abort?"

"Negative. Notify Romeo to take care of it."

"Roger."

Alex's brain was finally catching up to what was happening as he sat in the right seat while the detachment Officer-in-Charge flew the COD. *Talk about me being behind what the aircraft was doing. The SEAL was wearing a chute. Should've had time to pull the ripcord.* Alex looked down to the right and aft, but of course, it was dark.

"Altitude, altitude," the preset warning spoke into their helmets as Commander Sequera added some power and held the yoke steady to keep the aircraft nose high and AOA indicator steady as they approached the drop zone. The warning stopped as the C-2 rose above eight hundred feet.

The pilot fidgeted with his microphone, but it had stopped working. Instead, he looked to his right and yelled at Alex, "thirty-second

149

checklist." Lieutenant Commander Sequera slowed the twin-engine turboprop to ninety-five knots as they went through the checklist.

The airspeed warning flag appeared on the primary flight display. The rudder shakers activated, and Alex knew they were operating at the edge of the envelope just before a power-on stall. *Good thing I'm with the boss.*

Commander Sequera held the aircraft steady, nose high, until they heard the report, "Flight, Aft, SEAL team's all out."

Alex answered for the pilot, "Rog...."

A high-pitched voice from our aircrewman over the internal communications systems broke in before Alex could finish. "Flight, aft, we're taking small arms fire."

The pilot held the aircraft steady, advanced the power control to the stops, and raised the flaps. The plane was being willed to blast forward from its low and slow configuration, rapidly increasing airspeed to remove itself from immediate danger while holding its altitude.

Alex glanced at the primary flight display – one hundred fifteen knots, twenty-four degrees AOA, flaps coming up, and approaching zero. When he heard the rudder shakers again – they didn't stop as they did in training – he knew something was very, very wrong.

"Sir." Alex turned his head to the left only to witness Commander Sequera's helmet slumped forward in the seat to his left, eyes facing the deck, hands free of the controls. The aircraft shook, and the right-wing pitched up as the nose fell.

"Altitude, Altitude," the enunciating voice alerted the flight crew they were dangerously low.

Alex grabbed the yoke with his right hand, simultaneously slamming the power controls forward with his left. He twisted his body to support his right arm, using all his strength trying to raise the left wing. *Center the ball. Level the wings. Nose to the horizon.* The turbines howled, and the propellers bit into the cold Afghan night as they strained to keep the C-2 in the sky.

"Flight, Aft, we okay?"

Alex went over his actions in his head as he performed the following tasks. *Level the wings. Increase airspeed to one hundred thirty knots.*

Check rudder shakers have stopped. Leave the flaps up. Throttle back when safe.

"Flight, Aft, want me to raise the ramp?"

Again, Alex turned his head to check if the pilot was responsive. Lieutenant Commander Sequera remained slumped forward in his straps. "Sir...sir...." No response. "Aft, Flight. You okay back there?"

"Yes, sir."

"Good, leave the ramp alone, and come up here." Alex glanced back into the cargo compartment. "Commander Sequera is injured. Come up here and see what you can do." Alex pressed the mike switch, "Mayday, Mayday, Wild Stallion three two. Pilot unconscious. Small arms fire ...."

"Altitude, altitude."

Alex choked as the cockpit filled with small particles. The propellers shook. *God damn it. Can't talk and fly.* He slammed the power levers forward again and pulled back on the yoke. *Must've hit some treetops.* Yellow caution lights illuminated as the starboard turbine unwound and quit. Alex thrust the power lever again in a programmed response burned in his brain – the sudden loss of an engine. *Power levers forward, landing gear handle up, pull T-handle, fire button.* He looked out his windscreen; the starboard prop stopped and aligned with the slipstream – no fire. *Skip fire button, flaps one-third, left rudder, fuel dump.* Alex felt the crippled bird respond, and he saw the VSI show a positive rate of climb. The buzzing in his ears began to make sense.

The voice in his ears said, "Wild Stallion three two, this is Gremlin. Turn left, mountains to the east. Say the nature of your emergency."

Shit.

"Flight, Aft, sir, what's goin' on?"

Alex looked at Commander Sequera. He remained inert, a wet spot growing on the side of his flight suit.

"Flight, Aft, still want me to come up? Are we okay?" Donovan's voice warbled as he talked on the open microphone.

The aircraft continued to shake.

Props knocked out of balance.

The ground controller continued to talk to him, "Wild Stallion three two, come in."

Alex finally managed to say to his crewman back in the cargo compartment, "Aft, Flight, yes, get up here NOW."

"Roger."

The controller's voice was insistent and steady, "Wild Stallion three two, turn left – turn *port*, read back, over."

Alex eased the yoke and banked the aircraft into the remaining good engine. He set the aircraft's attitude with his yoke for the best single-engine rate of climb and, after regaining a northerly heading, raised the starboard wing to slip the plane through the night sky. The VSI still showed a positive rate of climb. Alex took a deep breath and exhaled slowly through pursed lips.

He shook his head and spoke into his microphone, "Gremlin, this is Wild Stallion three two. Roger turn port. Starboard engine out. Pilot unconscious and probably dead. Gimme a steer. Nearest divert."

"Roger Wild Stallion three two, your steer two seven zero, climb to five thousand feet...."

Alex didn't hear what followed. Instead, the aircraft shook even worse, the controls sluggish in his hands. The port turbine's ordinarily steady sounds fluctuated with increases and decreases that signaled the power plant developing about half its potential thrust. The VSI went from a climb through zero and showed a measurable descent. Alex could make out occasional lights on the ground, giving him some reference to the horizon.

"Altitude, altitude," the recorded voice issued a warning.

The power levers were already two-blocked forward – no additional thrust could be generated. "Aft, Flight, belay coming up. Get strapped in. Both engines out. We're going in."

"Aye," responded Donovan.

Alex scanned the ground and banked the aircraft to the left until he was headed one eight zero degrees. The radar altimeter read five hundred feet above the ground.

A jarring explosion of yellow light from the left and ahead of the plane was followed by tracer rounds zeroing in on the Navy transport.

A loud thud rocked the bird, and it shuddered as it fell off to the left. Smaller thumps struck the fuselage. The turbine and propellers quit straining and ended their heroic effort to keep Wild Stallion three two airborne. Particles again filled the cabin.

"Flight, Aft, looks like the port engine nacelle's been hit."

No longer needing to worry about battling asymmetrical power from one good engine, Alex first adjusted the nose to make sure they did not stall again and then went into a memorized routine for an over land double-engine failure.

Gear up, hydraulic isolation valve T/off and Land, flaps – one-third, blow ditching hatches, rudder–little into the windmilling prop, harness locked.

Alex stopped the fuel dump. As they glided to one hundred fifty feet, he raised the nose to steady the VSI at zero, twenty units AOA, wings level. He held his attitude as the aircraft flew down and forward until its inevitable reunion with *terra firma*.

Time slowed. *Okay, just like in the trainer.*

"Stand by for impact."

Dirt peppered the cockpit as the aircraft squatted and furrowed the rocky Afghan soil. Alex's mouth and nose filled with debris, and he gagged. The shriek of tearing metal knifed through the sound padding of his helmet, overriding all thought. He tried to control direction with his legs pushing on pedals and hands turning the yoke – but the rudder and ailerons were useless. Time slowed again as his vision tunneled to the flight controls and the instruments immediately in front.

Kerosene vapor burned his eyes and nostrils while his throat filled and chest tightened. All the air in his lungs exited through his clenched teeth as he involuntarily closed his eyes to blot out the images of destruction. Something wet hit his left cheek as the aircraft cocked violently to the right and continued to slide forward along the ground at an alarming forty-five-degree angle.

The aircraft bounced as it ran over uneven ground. Alex was jerked forward and to the left in his harness. His left shoulder smarted with a sharp pain causing him to lift his head and cry out, *"Madre Dios."*

The sounds of the fuselage crunching beneath his feet added to the noises of metal tearing. The acrid taste of bile rose in his throat. Alex opened his eyes to aircraft electronic boxes no longer arranged neatly on the instrument panel – a jungle of wires flying through the cockpit. Commander Sequera's helmet flew past, his head still inside, lips closed, sealing his last thoughts forever.

Alex's vision tunneled gray as his head throbbed and whipped from side to side.

As the aircraft slowed its slide across the Afghan soil …

… Alex sat up in bed, opened his eyes wide, and screamed.

*****

Jim Tritten is a retired Navy carrier pilot living in Corrales with his Danish author/artist wife Jasmine and four cats. He and Jasmine recently published *Kato's Grand Adventure, 2ⁿᵈ Ed*. He also recently published *Love and Lies: Call Me Eve* and *Panama's Gold*, both co-authored with Sandi Hoover.

Second Place   **Judith Castleberry**

The Gosling

At first, Liz walked just to get out of the house. Her empty home echoed with memories and yet was so silent that some days even the hum of the refrigerator seemed noisy. Carl, her husband, had died in the early days of the pandemic when people were still celebrating healthcare workers and abiding by the new restrictions.

Her children came anyway, driving from their distant homes to huddle in hers for a few days while they went through perfunctory rituals to mark Carl's death. The world was a fearful place where they couldn't even have the comfort of a public funeral, so they comforted each other as best they could. Somehow it had all felt so furtive, as if they had hidden this gracious man's death. He became just one more number, one more on the daily list of "man in his sixties with an underlying condition."

A few weeks after the children left and the tail-end of belated sympathy cards trickled to a stop, Liz found herself at loose ends on a bright spring afternoon. All the immediate things that needed to be done were tied up and what remained was too painful to consider. At some point she knew she needed to get rid of the rest of Carl's things, but for now, she just wasn't ready. So, she slipped on her walking shoes and headed for the river.

The city had created an interlapping series of walking trails between the cottonwoods that lined the river. For the most part, the trails and surrounding park was left in its natural state except for a few benches and a playground for children. During those early days, even the slides and swings were blocked off as no one knew if surfaces could carry the disease.

For weeks, then months, Liz walked the trails. She nodded and smiled at other walkers, or at least tried to under her mask. Her last image of Carl through the window of the ICU was seared in her brain. He no longer looked like her loving husband between the snarl of plastic tubing, surrounded by medical people covered head-to-toe in protective gear. No way she wanted to be responsible for someone else dying like that, so she maintained her distance and wore a mask. She could almost see the red spikey balls of disease hanging over people in the grocery store. Only the open trails, with lots of distance from other people felt safe.

As the seasons passed, Liz watched the ebb and flow of wildlife that inhabited the park. It was a safe space for deer, prairie dogs, and even skunks. The river attracted waterfowl, which in turn attracted small children with bags of stale popcorn or crackers, despite the many signs warning against feeding human food to wild animals.

The ducks and geese also ignored the signs, tending to gather at the spots most accessible to small children with treats. After dining, the birds wandered into the river, supplementing the children's offerings with bugs and algae. The Canada geese soar overhead in their distinctive vee formation. Other than the occasional territorial skirmish between the bands of geese, it was a peaceful life for the flocks of birds that called the riverine area home.

After a year of walks, it was an early spring day when Liz first encountered the mother goose and her three goslings. Momma goose led her little family across the path and down the bank to the river for a swim. Liz stepped closer, but the momma warned her away with a hiss. The goose had a white streak in the sleek black feathers above one eye giving her a startled expression which reminded Liz of an elderly aunt.

"Hattie, I won't bother your babies," Liz promised, bestowing the aunt's name on the goose.

*****

Today, a beautiful Saturday afternoon with a bright blue sky and trees the fresh green of early spring before they darken into summer, Liz parks her car at the outer edge of the small parking area. One of the first nice weekends in this dismal year has attracted more vehicles than usual.

156

On the dirt path under the arched cottonwoods, the regular walkers and runners are joined by family groups. Kids with brightly colored helmets wobble on bicycles, moms push strollers, and dads chase toddlers trying out their legs on the dirt path. Of course, there are the usual array of dogwalkers attached to canines of all sizes and varieties. Many of the dogwalkers are also regulars and Liz exchanges smiles and nods with them.

Past the playground, two tykes on scooters shoot toward Liz. She steps out of their way, as they don't seem to be aware of her. The parents trail about ten feet behind the scooters, the mom chatting loudly on a cell phone. The dad, a large man with a black tee shirt emblazoned with an eagle stretched across his wide belly, yells at the children to slow down, without any effect. Beside the man trots a pair of large dogs. Liz nods at them, but no one in the group seems to notice.

A noisy flock of geese swim and bob on the foamy dark river water. Liz imagines that their animated discussion is a commentary on the quantity of the spring runoff and the tastiness of the plant life in the river. Liz pauses when she notices Hattie and her goslings in a break between the bushes along the bank, lined up like debutants ready to make their first introduction into society.

"Sic 'em!" A human voice erupts in the din of geese voices.

Honks explode from the geese. Water churns as dozens of wings beat at it. The geese take to the sky. Right behind them race the two dogs she passed only moments before, the larger long-haired one struggling in the water.

"Sic 'em!" The large man hollers again.

The dogs shoot after their prey, but the geese are too swift, some of them already miles away in the azure sky. The dogs continue yelping after them for a moment then turn back toward their owner.

Liz freezes in place, only a few feet from the loud man, unable to move. She is shocked into silence by the suddenness and viciousness of the attack. The whole thing is over in seconds, the honks from the geese already fading in the distance.

The dogs scramble out of the water. The larger one has a mouthful of grey fluff that he deposits in front of the man. In horror, Liz realizes it is one of Hattie's goslings.

"What do you think you are doing?" Liz's feet thaw and she finds herself directly in front of the man.

"Aw, just havin' a little fun." The man smiles and shrugs.

"You killed it!" Liz points at the silent mound of fluff at his feet.

He nudges it with a sneaker. "It's probably just stunned." When the fluff doesn't move, he adds, "Anyway, it's just a goose."

The bright blue sky darkens, and all Liz can see is a red haze. A rage beyond anything she has felt in her entire life wells up inside her. Rage at this man shrugging away the death and destruction he has brought to this peaceful scene shakes her and she stutters as the words tumble out of her mouth, "And you're just a jackass!"

Then Liz does something that she has never done in her life, not even as a child. She balls up her fist and hits the man in his fat stomach, right below the eagle.

The blow doesn't make a dent on the broad expanse of tee shirt. For a moment, there is total silence.

"Are you crazy, lady?" The man takes a step back.

"I-I'm—" Reactively, Liz starts to apologize. What on earth has she done? Then she looks down at the pile of fluff at her feet and glares at the man. "I'm not crazy! This is not 'just a goose', it's Hattie's baby. How dare you sic your dogs on them!"

"Geez lady," the man shakes his head and looks around at the small crowd of Saturday afternoon walkers starting to gather. He turns and yells toward his wife, who has continued her loud conversation through the whole incident. "C'mon, let's go."

Without missing a word of her phone call, the wife motions toward her children and starts back down the trail toward the parking lot. The two little guys on scooters start to object, but their dad barks at them to get moving. He takes one last look over his shoulder at Liz and hustles down the path.

"Is the baby goose dead?" A brown-eyed little boy wearing a Paw Patrol tee shirt points at the pile of feathers.

"I don't know." Liz answers. She squats down to touch the still bird, but a loud hiss stops her.

Hattie, the mother goose, edges between Liz and her baby. Liz backs up quickly to give her room. Hattie pokes at the silent ball of fluff with her beak. She looks around at the humans and hisses angrily at them again. Then she is all mother, nudging the baby and preening its fluff. The other goslings huddle close, too, as if trying to warm their sibling.

"Are you all right?" A woman puts a protective arm around the little boy, but her sympathetic brown eyes focus on Liz.

Liz takes a deep breath, and it is like a dam gives way. Tears gush from her eyes with the intensity of the spring thaw on the river. She gulps, trying to speak.

The woman nods toward the goose. "Horrible what that man did. The animals here are so tame. Too tame really. They don't know they are supposed to be afraid of us."

Liz nods without speaking, fighting to control the onslaught of emotions. She is vaguely aware that a small circle of people is watching and commenting on the scene.

"Ought to call the cops on him."

"Aw, that one dog was a Chow. Don't you know they were bred for hunting?"

"There's a leash law in this park!"

"Do you think we should do something about the goose? Put it out of its misery?"

The brown-eyed woman leads Liz to a bench at the edge of the path. "Why don't you sit down for a minute."

Liz nods dumbly, unable to speak. She crumples to the seat and gasps, slowing the flow of tears. The woman sits next to her. The little boy leans on his mother's leg and stares at Liz.

"I apologize. I don't know why I went to pieces like that. I'm usually more in control." Liz digs in her jeans pocket for a tissue.

"That's all right."

"It's just—just—" Liz wipes at her eyes. "My husband died last year. I guess I'm still not dealing well with things."

"I'm so sorry." The woman lays her hand lightly on Liz's arm.

"Thanks." Liz dabs again at her eyes. "I don't mean to burden anyone. It's just been such a hard year."

"Yes." The woman sighs heavily. "My mother passed this year, too."

"I'm sorry." Liz reaches out and clasps the woman's hand.

There doesn't seem to be anything left to say and the two women drift into silence. The little boy wanders over to the few people still circled around Hattie and her babies.

"Mom! Mom!" The little boy speeds back to them. "The baby bird—it moved!"

The women jump to their feet and run the few steps to the baby goose. A man steps back to let them see.

Sure enough, the pile of fluff looks more like a gosling now, stretching its tiny head up toward Hattie. Hattie continues to preen its feathers as if to breathe strength into her baby.

"Will you look at that," the man says with a grin.

The gosling is trying to stand up on wobbly feet. Hattie steadies it with her beak as the other goslings watch.

"Don't touch it, it needs to get its bearings," a woman, wearing a straw sunhat, comments.

"That momma's not going to let you get close."

Slowly the gosling rises to its feet. Liz heart also rise in her chest. She holds her breath, willing the gosling to be all right.

"His wing." The boy's mother points.

The gosling stretches the stubby points of fluff at his sides that will one day grow into the magnificent wings of a Canada goose. But one of the wings doesn't stretch. It sticks out at an awkward angle.

"Oh." Liz's heart drops again.

Hattie continues to nudge the little creature, gently touching the broken wing. The baby takes a tentative step and Hattie makes a soft noise. The other goslings crowd in close. Together, the little group moves toward the river. Hattie nudges each baby into the river, the wounded one last. She stays close at its side and the whole family glides on the water.

"Aah," the cluster of humans on the bank seem to all sigh at once. They smile and nod at each other, relishing the shared moment before resuming their walks.

Soon, only Liz and the brown-eyed mother and son are left watching Hattie and her family swim.

"Mom, is the baby going to be all right?" The little boy asks.

"I think so." His mom replies. "His momma is going to take care of him."

Liz feels awkward, like she has forgotten what to do in the company of humans. "Um, thank you. You're very kind."

"I didn't do anything," the young mom protests.

"Yes, you did." Liz pauses again, still unsure what to say. "By the way, I'm Liz."

"I'm Rena. And this is Trey."

"Nice to meet you. Maybe I'll see you again, sometime."

"That would be great." Rena takes Trey's hand. "We moved here to be close to family, but with my mom—" she shakes her head.

"I'll be here tomorrow about the same time." Liz smiles down at Trey. "I'll bring some bird seed for the geese."

"Trey would really like that."

"See you then."

Trey waves and runs down the trail, Rena following him. Liz lingers to watch Hattie and her babies. The one with the broken wing is working hard to keep up and Hattie gently nudges him as if to encourage him along.

Liz smiles as she walks in the opposite direction, the warm sun unkinking the knots in her shoulders. She wonders if the pet store down the street has bird seed, and she will look for more information about the geese to share with Trey. Hattie is going to need a little help for her family to heal. For the first time in months, Liz finds herself looking forward to the next day.

*****

Judy Castleberry has written everything from grants to screenplays. Her screenplay *Office People* was recently selected to be produced by the Stagecoach Foundation at the Farmington Road Show. Stage plays include *Yard Sale*, *Villainy in the Valley*, and others. Judy is the author of *The Caregiver Zone* and has several unpublished novels

Third Place   **Jeffrey Otis**

The Lure of Flying

Daniel loved to fly. But not in airplanes, balloons, helicopters, rockets, or any of the other miraculous technologies commonplace in the 21st century.

His first flights began in his youth. When he was 13, a school bully punched him in the stomach, leaving him fearful and stressed. Later that day, the sight in his left eye went dark, and when it returned, everything was blue. He described it to his mother, who became alarmed and took him to the emergency room. By then, he had recovered.

The doctor said he had suffered a Transient Ischemic Attack or TIA. In plain terms, he had suffered a mini-stroke.

A year later, he was throwing a football with a friend after another rough day, full of missed assignments and awkward conversations with girls. Even worse, his teacher had sent him to the principal's office for passing a note to a friend which was read out loud to the class.

Daniel stood ready to throw. "Go out for a touchstone," he directed his friend.

He knew he'd said something strange, but couldn't figure out what it was. Instead of throwing the ball, Daniel sat in the grass, the ball rolling out of his hand, his blue eyes gazing vacantly at the ground. His next memory was of people looking at him from above, asking questions.

The apparent strokes persisted.

Daniel's 11th grade English teacher liked to call on students to read out loud from the textbook.

"Daniel, please read the first stanza of Wordsworth's poem," she said.

Daniel hated being called on.

He stared at the page, saw the letters, the commas, but didn't know what the symbols meant. He could speak, understand the teacher's words, he just couldn't read. Now, his blood pushed into his cheeks in hot waves, a mix of shame and something else. But that feeling was soon immaterial, replaced by wonder at what his eyes saw. Tiny holes on the page widened, revealing purple blossoms that moved in unison like seaweed bending with the surf. The air smelled of mint. He found himself floating, freed from the heavy hold of the world.

The doctors informed him and his parents he was at high risk for a massive, debilitating stroke that might leave him paralyzed, without short-term memory, or dead. But Daniel's lack of any risk factors for stroke puzzled the doctors. He had low blood pressure, low cholesterol, no heart problems, no diabetes, and he didn't smoke. The hallucinations were unusual, so they ran tests for a tumor, but none showed on the x-rays.

Daniel earned a Ph.D. in ecology and taught at the University of New Mexico, where he married a petite colleague with a beautiful mind and poetic name. Song's English was so precise a blind man could easily fail to recognize her as an immigrant from Taiwan.

When Daniel returned from a conference in Colorado centered on deforestation, he shared what he'd learned with Song. They relaxed and talked as they drank her favorite tea.

"I wish I could have come. Maybe next time." Song smiled, flicking her black bangs to the side as she fingered the delicate gold dragon that hung from her necklace, one of the few pieces of jewelry she wore.

"I had another episode back in my room," Daniel said. "I was feeling down after listening to several talks about the crisis in the Amazon. As I lay on the bed, I heard jungle trees speaking to me. They cried a slow wail measured in years. The forest was withering, and I felt so badly I flew away using beautiful wings that unfurled from my back. My feathers were creamy white with golden tips. When I came to, the forest's moans continued for several minutes."

"These things aren't strokes. I don't care what the doctors say. These episodes are a kind of… well, a psychotic thing. You really need medication for this, Daniel."

"I just think my brain gets tired. Once I've rested, the problem goes away."

"Well, I worry, Daniel." Song put her small hand on his tanned arm.

"I know. Maybe with your help, I might control the hallucinations, fight them," he said somewhat passively.

"Daniel, it's one thing to check out occasionally, but please don't check out to the point you never come back. I need you here."

That week, the wildfires began. The land and sky had nothing to offer the thirsty grasses and gnarled trees and they succumbed to a spark. The study area where Daniel did his research went up in flames, bringing his plans to an end.

On the evening the fires reached their maximum extent, Daniel sat in his easy chair, exhausted.

As he rested, he sensed a cool wave of air wash over him and noticed the front door slowly open, letting in the garden roses. The branches grew along the contours of the entryway, producing a chorus of gentle harmonies and hinting at colors he'd never seen before. Beneath him came the distant sound of drums. Light now emanated from the palms of his hands. As he looked deeper into them, he was gently transported out beyond the confines of his home and into the rich, aromatic forest of a tranquil land.

A brilliant emerald fell from a branch into his open palm. He could see it was alive but trapped within its crystal. He closed his hand over it. When it opened, rivers of playful green light flowed outward and upward, curving and carrying speckles of shimmering starlight. At the end of each river, a bird emerged full of color and delight, fluttering above him as if waiting for him to follow. He felt his shirt tear as his wings broke free and he joined the birds. It was all so beautiful. So beautiful. Beautiful...

A small, distant voice whispered, "Come back now. You're in danger." He felt a struggle forming within himself.

Gradually, the light faded, the birds flew away, and Daniel was back in his easy chair. *I love such wonders*, he thought. He wanted to stay in that world of magic forever. Like Ulysses, he had seen the Sirens, heard their sweet song, and lived to tell of it. Soon he slept.

His psychosis was breaking through the meds.

Months later, Daniel watched on TV as Russian tanks rolled into Ukraine. The people on the street were bloodied and dazed, and a pregnant woman lay on a stretcher.

He had to get out of the house, breathe some fresh air. He stood on the porch, squinting at the sun.

A strange odor filled his nostrils like oranges mixed with lilacs. Before he could look around for the source, he lost all vision. He fell, grasping for something to hold on to, and gashed one knee.

When his vision returned, he saw the soldiers. Why were soldiers nearby? They laughed as they cleaned their guns. But they had reptilian scales on their hands.

One got up and stood over him, nudging him with his rifle. Daniel felt a familiar surge of movement in his back. His shirt ripped as wings emerged, filled with the energy that birthed a universe.

As the huge appendages fully extended, he stood, and soon his legs were no longer on the ground. The soldier looked puzzled as Daniel moved through the air with each whooshing stroke of the powerful wings, looking down as he flew up and back, facing the man. Once he reached tree height, he paused, studied the soldier, then turned toward the crystal mountains with their twisting water spouts.

When he woke, it was late. He heard Song call his name.

"I'm fine," he told her. "I fell and hurt my knee, that's all."

Song looked at him askance. "I don't believe you. And why do you keep moving your shoulders?"

"I had another episode," he confessed.

"Oh, Daniel. Are you alright? Perhaps you need stronger meds."

"I should go to bed. I'm so tired," he said, then paused. "You know, maybe I'm not really ill anymore."

Song looked at him quizzically.

He took her hand. "I need to leave the world to be in the world." Looking at her with wide eyes, he whispered, "Today I flew."

Daniel had to take a sabbatical from teaching. His episodes were increasing in frequency and duration. After a year, the university let him go.

Soon, Song learned that he'd stopped taking his meds.

"I don't like the way the pills make me feel," he said to her.

"Imagine how I feel when you don't take them. They don't make you ill or cause any bad side-effects that I can see."

"The world is a bad side-effect," he grumbled.

"Daniel, I'm part of the world. I need you to take the pills. It isn't fair to me or you if you don't."

He managed to take his meds for another two years.

The schools always needed substitute teachers, and he became one. The pay was low, but the job got him out of the house and put him amongst young people.

Students were experts at getting subs off track. In Daniel's case, he talked about the importance of following your dreams.

"You need to find the thing you're good at, or the thing that gives you great pleasure, and pursue it."

"Yeah, Jake here is really good at that," a student said, causing a ripple of laughter from the class.

Daniel noticed Jake was laughing louder than anyone.

Then the principal's voice came over the speaker on the wall. "Teachers, we are on lockdown. Move your students against the walls away from the windows, shut off the lights, lock all doors and remain silent. I repeat…"

Another drill, Daniel thought. Then he saw a boy with a gun walk past the small window of the door to the classroom. The boy didn't stop and continued purposefully down the hall. That day, the shooter and another student died.

Daniel stopped taking his meds.

His relationship with Song deteriorated as a result. In a twisted sort of logic, it was all the more reason, in Daniel's mind, to flee to an alternate reality. He felt selfish and unfaithful to her, yet he could only find relief in his episodes. The more he hated himself for the pain he caused her, the more he wanted to escape. The more he wanted to escape, the more often the illusions came.

The other worlds drew him in until he forgot the world he had come from. Now he permanently inhabited a land filled with wonder, a place where massive ships of strange design entered the atmosphere and hovered miles above him, twinkling and making a faint hum as their engines moved them in a stately arc across the sky.

They never touched the ground; they didn't interfere. Daniel yearned to meet the visitors and be part of their dream.

There was always something out there that was beyond his grasp.

But today he flew.

He flew over majestic mountains whose blue glaciers cooled the air above them.

He flew over herds of mammoths grazing along the lush slopes.

He flew over places with houses inside hillsides covered in grass.

Daniel flew on until the light faded and the beautiful memories dissolved.

*****

Jeff Otis. Reading has always been one of my passions and in 2020 I took up writing. I have two novels that are essentially complete in the science fiction/action-adventure genre that I am hoping to publish soon. A third novel is in progress.

Section Nine

Prose – Voyages

The second prose category could be a voyage through time, memory and/or physical location. The vehicle did not have to be a boat or a spaceship, but it did have to have a travel component.

All the best stories engage the reader's emotions as well as their minds. Here are three stories with very different viewpoints and attitudes.

First Place   **Evelyn Neil**

Hitch Hiker

His mind a jumble of conflicting memories, Ken whistled along to John Denver's Country Roads Take Me Home on the radio and negotiated the curves through Tijeras Canyon. In high spirits, he was headed home to Kansas for the Holidays for the first time in fifteen years. After this long, he still felt guilty for abandoning his parents and the family farm after coming home from Vietnam. But he'd needed to escape the persistent questions that spawned the nightmares of mud, blood, cries of wounded comrades and the stench of death. "What was it like over there? What happened to erase the twinkle from his eye and render him so quiet? Was he there when his cousin Davy died?" So many questions about things he wanted to forget.

So west was the direction he'd taken as far as Albuquerque where no one knew him. There he found employment driving a truck towing a manure spreader. He spent long days shoveling manure from the stock pens at Valley Gold Dairy and Karler Packing Company in the South Valley and spreading it on the North Valley alfalfa fields irrigated by water from the Rio Grande. This manual labor in the out-of-doors quieted his mind.

With very little traffic on this winter morning, the ride was pleasant and uneventful. Ken stopped in Santa Rosa to top off the gas tank of his new 1993 F-150 and to stretch his legs. The brisk wind from the eastern plains cut through his red and black plaid shirt and tugged at his black Stetson. The gray New Mexico sky promised rain, maybe even snow.

A few miles east of Tucumcari, Ken whipped the pickup onto the shoulder at the sight of a hitchhiker in an olive-drab dress uniform. The soldier, who resembled Davy, lowered his right thumb, picked up a canvas tote and sprinted to the truck. Ken leaned his stout body across the seat and shouted out the passenger window.

"Where're you headed, son?"

"Kansas City," the shivering young man responded.

"That's close to where I'm headed. Hop in." Ken observed how loose the uniform hung on the young serviceman.

"Thanks, it's really cold out there." The stranger climbed in and clutched the tan bag on his lap. He wiped his nose with the back of his hand, tossed his hat onto the dash and ran grimy fingers through his cropped ginger hair. His teeth chattered as he fidgeted with the bag.

Ken turned up the heater. "We'll get you warmed up in no time." He reached into his new denim bibs and extracted a pack of Marlboros. "Cigarette?"

"Uh, no thanks."

"Mind if I have one?"

"No......no, not at all."

Ken took a long drag and exhaled slowly. With steely blue eyes he surveyed his red-eyed, pimply-faced passenger. The patch of the 226 Signal Company on the left sleeve of the jacket caught his eye. Realizing this kid was wearing an old uniform with an outdated Korea era unit patch, he asked, "Where've you served?"

"Oh uh, here and there." The kid reached into the bag and pulled out a Smith and Wesson .38 and pressed the cold steel barrel of the revolver into Ken's temple. "Pull over. I need this truck."

"Over my dead body." Ken spat the cigarette to the floor, clenched his teeth and stomped on the accelerator. The speedometer needle climbed----seventy, eighty, ninety-five.

"Hey man, slow down. You're gonna kill us." The stench of sweat and fear filled the over-heated cab.

"Go ahead! Pull the trigger." Ken yelled. "We can go together."

"Please, mister," sniffled the kid. "I don't wanna die."

The needle held steady at ninety-five.

"Okay, tell you what. Roll down your window. Toss out the weapon."

The cold December air rushed into the cab as the gun sailed into the barrow pit racing away from them. They continued to fly over the uneven pavement, around curves and over bridges. As he swerved around slower moving vehicles and struggled to maintain his calm, Ken longed for the flashing red lights of a black and white cruiser.

"Now, you damned imposter, take off the uniform. Toss it out."

The shaking youngster wriggled out of the wool jacket. Out the window it flew down the highway behind the speeding Ford like a run-a-way kite. Next out was the tie and shirt.

"Now the shoes and socks. And pants, too," demanded Ken.

"Oh, man. Slow down."

Ken slowed the truck and pulled it onto the side of the road. The kid gasped with relief and leaned his head against the passenger window.

"Get your sorry ass outta my truck," commanded Ken. "Oh, and take that hat and filthy tote with you."

"But, I'll freeze out there," the nearly naked kid whined.

"That's the general idea, you little son-of-a-bitch."

Ken put the truck into gear. Spinning out and kicking up gravel, he pulled onto I-40 and turned up the radio. "Teach him to disrespect the uniform," he muttered as he looked in the rear view mirror to see the hitchhiker in his wind-swept boxers wildly searching the barren landscape.

*****

Evelyn Neil, an award-winning author, began writing following retirement from a career as a small business owner/accountant. Her short stories appear regularly in anthologies and journals. Her memoir, *DANCING TO THE END OF OUR RAINBOW*, an indelible tale of love, despair and discovery explores end-of-life choices and is available on Amazon.com. Learn more on www.rmkpublications.com/evelyn-neil

Second Place   **Patricia Walkow**

An Unexpected Voyage

It sounded like a good idea, at least on paper. Enchanting color photos and italic script graced the captivating travel brochure:

"Extend your visit to Peru. After seeing the cultural and historic treasures at Cusco and Machu Picchu, explore the country's wild side and see nature at its most pure in the Peruvian Amazon. Your Amazon adventure begins at the equatorial river port of Iquitos, where you will travel by boat to your deep jungle lodge and experience life in the Amazon first-hand."

Peru had been a dream of mine, and the Amazon was certainly on my list of places to see. I planned to visit when I was old, and "old" meant forty. Besides, a trip to the Amazon affords the traveler a certain level of bragging rights. The dream included my husband, Walter. But he had no interest in this particular trip.

I was disappointed, but I still booked a tour that included just a few other travelers.

Off I flew to Lima, then Cusco high in the stark Alta Plano of the Andes, to lush Machu Picchu, and finally to Iquitos, an Amazon port. At Iquitos, the humidity averaged 115 percent.

It sounded like a good idea when I read the brochure at home.

The morning after we arrived at Iquitos, my tour group boarded a metal dugout-style boat, about thirty feet long. There was a palm-thatched canopy shading part of the boat, and as the engine started, the movement generated a welcome breeze.

The river twisted and turned and seemed to get lost among its peninsulas and islands, eventually finding its main channel once again. It reminded me of an endless pretzel, a hopeless landscape. No mountains, no sense of direction, as close to lost as I had ever been—

and that was with a guide. I wondered if I would ever be able to find my way out of there if I had to.

Laughing mocha-colored children cavorted on the riverbank, playing, screaming, teasing, as children do everywhere. Some of them swam, others tried fishing. Mothers washed clothing from colorful plastic buckets.

"Walter, why aren't you here to see this?"

Our lodge, downriver for over an hour, would not have electricity and I felt game for the adventure.

Finally, we alit on a dark, wet beach. Our shoes sunk to the laces in thick spongy mush, causing a sucking vacuum sound with each step we took to walk up to the lodge, a few hundred feet inland. It sat on stilts on a low rise above the water.

As my shoes dried to a gritty matte brown, I recalled it had sounded like a good idea to visit the Amazon.

Immediately, I recognized Iquitos seemed less humid than here at the lodge. I didn't think that was possible.

Also, I was completely lost. I knew I was on the planet and the continent of South America, but I knew little else and recalled a line from the brochure:

"...travel by boat to your unique, secluded deep jungle lodge..."

The thatched lodge itself was fascinating, but our first order of business was to visit a local village to barter with the inhabitants.

It appears I had failed to read the part of the brochure about trading and was woefully unprepared for any exchange. But the crafts the children made were too good to pass up and I scrounged in my satchel for anything I thought they might like to have. Taking a gamble, I emptied a blue Estée Lauder waterproof makeup case and held it high in the air, demonstrating how the zipper worked. Immediately, seven arms went up, each offering something to trade. I selected a ceremonial (non-functional) blowgun, wrapped in ocelot fur and bearing long pointed darts with needle-sharp tips.

175

The rest of the afternoon was spent in my handwoven hammock, safely suspended from some posts under a straw pavilion at our lodge. I tried to sleep, but I quickly learned a body resting on a hammock attracted beetles. And apparently, they laughed at DEET. What I didn't yet know was those beetles were just the small ones.

Sunset comes early near the equator, and before long we were called to supper on the expansive dining veranda. We sat four or six at a table and enjoyed a simple, fresh meal of fish, vegetables, and fruit.

As daylight waned, beetles crawled over our table, up our legs, clinging to our skin or slacks. Flying insects whacked our necks. I had to guard my food so they wouldn't crawl into it. But I had lost my appetite, so I didn't care.

"... you will travel by boat to your deep jungle lodge and experience life in the Amazon first-hand..."

It had sounded like a good idea on paper.

That night, eerie shadows cast by my kerosene light danced on the dark wooden slats serving as walls in my cabin. I quickly sponge-bathed with a washcloth and bottled water and attempted to dry myself with a towel. Towel drying is nearly impossible where the humidity is so high. After lathering myself in insecticide, I shook out my nightgown to be sure there was nothing alive inside. As I reclined on the bed, it occurred to me a mattress is a foolish thing in the tropics. It is hot, sticky, and wet, and only heaven knows what was living in it. I lay sweating on the bed, covered in DEET, almost panicked.

It was too hot. I couldn't sleep. There wasn't enough air. It was noisy. Every creature that could make noise was making it. After lying in bed, sweating still, I heard a new noise.

THWACK!

What was that?

I was too afraid to pull back the curtains and discover something grotesque; too anxious to even touch the curtain; too wary to put my foot on the floor.

THWACK!

God!

That was enough. I jumped into my shoes, horrified I didn't check them for creatures first, and gingerly pulled aside the curtain. There, at eye level, I came face-to-face with the underbelly of a huge bat. Some hapless critter was in its maw.

I opened another curtain. Another bat. Another midnight snack.

It had sounded like a good idea.

"...Why not explore the wild side and see nature at its most pure?"

I realized I was no longer on a vacation, but rather, on a physical and mental voyage to a place so alien to me that I might as well learn from it. But I had experienced about all I could stand of nature for one night.

The next morning, we hiked about one-quarter mile from the river to an inland black water lake. It was only a few acres wide, and we boarded small, hand-made wooden dugouts. There wasn't a breath of air. It was the definition of "stagnant." Hot. Humid. Pungent. Still. Once we reached the middle of the lake, the boat's paddler handed each of the three guests in the boat a rather short twig of a fishing line with a tiny nub of some kind of bait suspended from some twine. We were told to see what we could catch.

I gamely did as I was told and was the first to catch a fish. At about six inches across and eight inches long, it wasn't too large and was somewhat translucent with tinges of orange. Its teeth were big and needle-sharp.

My first piranha.

Do you mean we are sitting in a tiny, tippy wooden canoe in a lake filled with piranha?

A young boy in a canoe glided toward us. He helped me remove the fish from the pole, and I let him keep my catch. We were told the locals skewer and roast them until crunchy.

He re-baited my line. Ten seconds later, I had nailed another piranha. So had everyone else in my boat.

The heat must have been getting to me. I sat there in the boat, stupefied. I may as well have been drugged. *What if I stick my finger in the water? Suppose I do that?*

When we left the lake I dallied a bit, preferring to remain at the tail end of our group with one of the guides as the rest of the group headed back toward the river. I walked only slightly ahead of the guide.

"Miss, will you please stay still for a moment?" he asked.

I stopped and turned my head.

"Yes, why?"

"Do not be alarmed. A snake is approaching from your right, a few feet in front of you. It won't bother you, I think. It's large. Just let it pass."

I froze. I like snakes, but don't know them, so I am cautious around them.

The snake slithered about ten feet in front of me. It stopped for a moment, raised its head and flicked its tongue, as though to check me out, and continued past me. And then it continued to pass me some more.

"What is it?" I asked the guide.

"A constrictor. A big one. Maybe fifteen feet."

It had sounded like a good idea.

Walter, you won't believe what just happened.

My bragging rights about this trip continued to expand. No…not a trip. A journey outside my zone of comfort.

When I retired for the evening, the same animal-kingdom ruckus as the previous night accompanied me as I tried to sleep. I was not as anxious, though, until I had to get up, put my shoes on, and head to the bathroom in my cabin to urinate.

There, on the dark wood wall behind the toilet was a beetle about two inches long, pointed uphill. I shined my flashlight on it. It was pale brown, with iridescent blue and green stripes. Pretty, actually. But I couldn't take the chance of having it fall—or worse—fly into me when my back was to it.

I went back to bed.

But I had to pee!

I got up again and gently swatted it with a towel. It fell on the floor. Now I couldn't find it and that was far worse than just having it on the wall behind me. Now I REALLY couldn't pee.

Back to bed.

It didn't work. I returned to the bathroom and engaged in what could only be described as speed-peeing.

It had sounded like a good idea.

Rain awakened me in the middle of the night. It silenced all the screaming creatures. I turned over in bed, pulled aside the curtain on the window above my head, and through the waning light of each cabin's light, witnessed rain falling straighter than I had ever seen it fall before. Then, it stopped. Drums beat in the distance. And to my disbelief, it became more humid.

What if I never get out of here?

I sat up and started to sob. *Why did I ever come here?*

With time, I learned to see my Amazon experience more objectively. Or maybe, it just isn't raw any longer.

My brief encounter with a climate and terrain so unfamiliar to me shattered my smugness and shoved me light years beyond anything I had encountered until that time. It identified fears I didn't know I had and exposed the joy I felt at the exotic experiences I enjoyed.

But isn't that what a journey is sometimes supposed to do...take you on an unexpected voyage into unusual corners of the world and unchartered recesses of your psyche?

And yes, it was a good idea.

*****

As both an author in multiple genres and an editor, **Patricia Walkow** is a member of many writing organizations and a founding member of the Corrales [New Mexico] Writing Group. Her full-length books, editing, and short stories have won multiple national or international awards. She has co-authored a mystery/romance and recently signed a contract to have it published in 2023

Third Place   **Jette Tritten**

Across the Atlantic

The Sea cures all ailments of man.
~ Plato

A dream or reality? Like a Nordic Viking Queen, I stood on the top deck of the Norwegian ocean liner, *Bergensfjord*, in the summer breeze, clutching Dannebrog – the Danish flag – in my right fist, ready to conquer the world. My armor? A cobalt blue skirt and jacket my mother had sewn with a matching, blue-dotted blouse, and white gloves she made me wear to protect the sensitive skin of my hands. The chilly wind blew through my blonde hair and erased memories of a time gone by. I had made the leap and headed into the unknown.

Family and friends clumped together on the quay of *Langelinie,* in the port of Copenhagen, near the famous statue of the Little Mermaid. They threw flowers my way, I heard laughter and cries simultaneously, and they swung flags, scarves, balloons, handkerchiefs, or signs with BON VOYAGE. While waving my arms back and forth with the Danish flag tight in my hand, I fought the tears and my stomach shuddered.

Never had I traveled on a large ship across the big ocean to another part of the world. But I remember having sailed in boats from Denmark to England, Germany, and Norway besides taking small ferries between the islands of my home country. However, nothing measured up to this voyage. My life would never be the same again. While bouncing from one foot to the other my heart raced in my chest. Next to me stood my Danish friend Lis, a schoolmate of mine, who at the last moment joined me in this adventure.

The amazing *Bergensfjord* happened to be one of the last transatlantic ocean liners in 1964 sailing from Copenhagen via Oslo to New York. Of the 878 passengers onboard, more than half were immigrants, including Lis and me. From the mid-sixties on, people who desired to travel from Copenhagen to America, flew by airplane straight to New York. Our ship appeared small and quaint compared to the gigantic cruise ships currently floating around every corner of the world containing 3,000-6,000 passengers. But not for me! I had never sailed in such an enormous vessel.

The ocean liner pulled away from my home country and set course to a new world. Fresh sea air saturated my nose and lungs and the loud band music faded from my ears. As the ship sailed further and further away from the dock, people gradually became smaller and smaller, turning into tiny dots in all colors of the rainbow until they became a big blur. I strained my eyes to get a last glimpse of them, then tears rolled down my cheeks from the excitement and exhilaration. Part of me felt sad because I still loved my family and friends. When would I ever see them again?

At that moment, saying goodbye to a world of twenty-one years became more difficult than anticipated. In hindsight, I left Denmark determined to experience other cultures and for adventure. My gut told me to leave, not my logical mind. While justifying my actions, Lis nudged me in the side and brought me back to reality. Glad she decided to come along after all.

Rays of the morning sun sparkled and danced on the surface of the ocean. I stared into the deep blue water rippling in a rhythmic pattern and then pulled off the white gloves from my hands. One at a time, I threw them into the rolling waves and watched them disappear. *The sea monster swallowed them. What a relief. Hurrah! I am free, free to be me. Free from my mother and her influence.* I leaned back my head, lifted my arms high and took in a deep breath, filling my lungs to their full capacity with the salty air from the sea.

Of course, I loved my mother, but needed to get away from her, as far away as possible, out of her clutch. My goal? San Francisco on the other side of the earth seemed like the perfect distance from Denmark. *I am now in control of my own future.* The vessel and ocean in front of my eyes steered me toward my destiny, whatever that might be. With an embroidered, ivory colored handkerchief I wiped away my tears, leaned towards Lis and said, "Do you think we'll ever return?"

She did not answer me right away. For a while we watched the waves splash as we walked along the side of the ship and looked back a last time at the country we had left behind. Cool mist from the white tops landed in my face, refreshed me, and cleared my head. Lis turned in my direction and said,

"Let's celebrate our freedom and our home for the next ten days." So, we headed down below into our cabin, lowered ourselves into small chairs, and gulped a shot of *aquavit* Lis brought. The potent liquid quickly ran through and warmed my body all the way to my toes, calming my emotions. I lay down and relaxed in the lower bunk bed.

Despite my dream finally coming true, tears welled up in my eyes, when I realized the monumental decision, I had made. *I wonder if I did the right thing.* Earlier in Denmark when I told my mother about my life-changing plans, she said to me, "Even if I don't like it, I would rather you go to America and be happy, than stay here unhappy." She gave me the green light to go. Forever I will remember her for that gift and have thanked her repeatedly ever since.

The next couple of days, we explored every square inch of the ship. Each time I walked along the decks on the outside and my eyes glanced at the shimmering surface of the cobalt blue water I felt invigorated. At the same time, as I gazed into the rolling waves, a healing took effect on my inner wounds and traumas, especially the trauma of my father's death when I was twelve years old…when my entire world collapsed. Here in the depth of the blues and foam of the ocean the buried feelings of despair drowned and dissipated.

As I leaned over the railing late one afternoon, my eyes skimmed over the white-topped surface towards the western horizon where the deep red setting sun cast its golden rays upon the sky. Thoughts and dreams of what awaited us in America swirled through my mind. Soon I would be in a different world. *How did the Vikings ever make it across the Atlantic Ocean in tiny boats with sails and oars? How many did not make it?*

Seagulls followed our ship. From the top deck, I threw pieces of leftover bread from our meals up into the sky and the gulls swooped around to catch them midair with their beaks. Each time I spotted gray and white Dolphins jump out of the water in front of the ship, I smiled. Gazing down into the darkness, I heard Frank Sinatra's voice singing "How Deep is the Ocean" repeatedly. I pondered the amount of Eiffel towers on top of each other it would take before reaching the bottom. The secrets of the sea stayed concealed. *I wonder the number of sunken ships with treasures lay underneath the surface, deep down at the bottom.*

When not with Lis, I sat on a bench outside on one of the top decks wrapped in a blanket and stared into the vastness, letting my imagination take me into another realm. *Maybe I will see the fin of a shark, or a whale jump out of the water.* I made up stories in my mind about what happened above the surface and about what took place beneath with fish and plants.

Often "The Little Mermaid" fairy tale by fellow Dane, Hans Christian Andersen, popped into my head. As a child, I sat on my father's knee while he read aloud about her adventures from under the sea. I still remember vividly two etchings of her from the leatherbound volume with her fishtail full of barnacles wrapped around seaweed at the bottom. *There is an entire world underneath the surface.* So, I fantasized about the bottom of the ocean. Fear never overwhelmed me during the long cruise. Like a true Viking I remained fearless and courageous.

Two young, naive, Danish, blue-eyed, blonde girls like Lis and me continuously had fun on the huge ship, even if most passengers were the same age as our grandparents. How could we help but flirt with the good-looking Norwegian crew onboard? Learning to say "no" to the constant offerings of drinks, became our biggest challenge. Besides refusing to indulge in the spreads of delicious Norwegian food served buffet style three times a day. When getting a whiff of smoked salmon or the strong aroma of European cheeses at the breakfast buffet, how could we resist the temptation?

To justify our ferocious appetites, we promenaded back and forth on the decks at all hours of the day. We dove into the large pool and swam unlimited laps to keep off the calories and used exercise machines in the gym. Every evening, the band played, and we danced our feet off. I pulled out on the dance floor each willing person to practice what I learned in Denmark of social dance, folk dance, or ballroom dance. The days ended singing with fellow Danes, songs we learned in our childhood, a treasured part of the Danish culture. *Would we remember our heritage, or might it become replaced with our new life in America?*

Then, suddenly a raging storm, like a hurricane, surprised us. For three days the ship rolled from one side to the other in waves as tall as two-story buildings. Half of the passengers became seasick and threw up. Most people stayed in their cabins dreadfully ill. Vomit boxes appeared everywhere. An unbearable stench filled the passageways and compartments, enough to make a person sick, even if you were not. The crew tied down tables and chairs. Rubber runners covered the floors to prevent people from sliding.

"We must stay strong through this," I hinted to Lis, determined not to give in to sickness. In that moment I truly felt like a Viking on my first voyage, embracing every moment whether good or bad. During the height of the storm, we stayed safe in our cabin, located mid-ship, lying down, holding on to our bunk beds. Earlier, I brought food to our cabin, enough to sustain us for a couple of days.

Glad we had no window in our space. Unless we happened to be acrobats, walking around anywhere outside became impossible. Loud sounds hit our ears of crashing waves and objects flying, hitting whatever. Miraculously, we survived without getting ill or hurt. Must be our good Nordic genes.

After the horrendous storm everything became tranquil onboard for a couple of days. People slowly recovered from the tumultuous experience. Immediately, I went for a stroll on the freshly washed deck outside, stared into the relative calm water stretching as far as my eyes reached, into eternity, and thanked God for sparing us.

At sunrise as the fire red sun slowly ascended, the intoxicating smell of the ocean and the sound of waves crashing against the bow hypnotized me and brought back memories. Thoughts went back to my childhood when I watched the straight between Denmark and Sweden from my room in the villa where I lived the first twelve years of my life. I grew up next to water in which we swam and went sailing in the summer and ice skated in the winter, frequently in stormy weather.

About nine days passed, when in the long distance I spotted land, what looked like tall skyscrapers. As *Bergensfjord* approached New York City, my heart throbbed, and I smiled from one ear to the other. A big moment had arrived for this dream of mine. Our ship sailed up the Hudson River at sunset. We rushed straight up on the upper deck. With arms in the air and my lungs at full capacity I screamed,

"Hurrah, America, we are finally here!" People stared, but I did not care.

A red glow filled the evening sky and slowly changed into different shades of purple. Soon it darkened, and lights shined from all the buildings like stars. In awe, we reached for the luminosities but had to stay onboard until the following morning. Our ship slowly lowered its anchor for the night. *Cannot wait.* Hardly closed an eye. But we had one more hurdle before reaching land - before the end of our voyage.

Early the next morning, the lengthy process of entering the U.S. as immigrants began.

Negative thoughts bombarded my head. *What if the Immigration and Naturalization officers do not accept us? They could refuse our entry and send us back to Denmark. The X-rays might show a spot on the lung suspicious of Tuberculosis. If we have visited The Soviet Union, been in jail or for whatever reason, they can just say "no."*

After standing in line for five hours onboard the ship to get on land in New York Harbor, my legs tired and my stomach quivered. Sweat dribbled down my back in the summer heat. I kept biting the insides of my cheeks until they bled. Under my left arm I carried a large, yellow, sealed envelope containing two chest X-rays. The bag over my right shoulder bulged with papers required for entry. For eight months prior to the trip, I went back and forth to process them at the American Embassy in Copenhagen.

Finally, my turn came. With a raising heart beat I stepped forward towards the immigration officer and smiled. Quickly he checked through my papers and X-rays without a word, and with a nod, let me go through. I sighed in relief and rubbed my tender shoulder muscles. *I cannot believe I went through already.*

Next in line, my friend Lis. The officer gazed at her papers, then lifted her X-rays up into the light. He rotated them, carefully examining every section from one side to the other. *Will he let her pass?* He frowned, pointed his finger to a spot on one of the X-rays and remarked,

"Something looks suspicious on the lung right there." I cringed. Lis spoke up at once, her voice shaking,

"I have had pneumonia twice, and it left scar tissue. That is what you see."

Surprised, the officer stared at her and examined the X-rays thoroughly one more time. Then he handed them back to her and shouted, "Okay, next person!" The sound of his loud voice hurt my ears, but we were free to go. *Yahoo! I cannot believe it is true.*

Grateful and relieved, we jumped up and down, each with a GREEN CARD in hand. After gathering papers and luggage we stepped triumphantly upon land while repeatedly shouting, "Hurrah, America, here we come."

From that time on, we had legal permission to stay in the U.S. for an unlimited time, on the condition we behaved ourselves. No more did we need to worry about falling in love with somebody and then having to leave the country after a certain period. The struggle had been long, with hurdles to overcome, but at last I was free to create my own life, free to be myself.

For years I lived an adventurous life in California and traveled around the world before I connected with my mother again. Despite living on opposite sides of the earth, we became closer than ever through letters and telephone conversations and repaired our once distraught relationship. To this day, I remain grateful she let me break free from her, from my home country and let me travel across the Atlantic Ocean toward my goal in America.

*****

Jasmine (Jette) Tritten is an award-winning author residing in New Mexico. She has written numerous short stories, and published a memoir *The Journey of an Adventuresome Dane* in 2015. In 2020, Jasmine published *On the Nile with a Dancing Dane*. She wrote a children's story *Kato's Grand Adventure* with her husband, published in 2021

Sandia Mountains
Photograph by Jette Tritten

Section Ten

Prose – Mountains

Mountains can be large piles of earth and rock, or they can be an overwhelming problem one has to deal with. Mountains can inspire us.

Again, we have three different interpretations of what and how a mountain will affect a person in these award winning stories.

First Place   **Leonie Rosenstiel**

Creative Procrastination

Sitting alone in his office, frustrated, Anthony knew the deadline was more than creeping up on him. He had to file that pleading by next Friday. *Had* to write it. He'd tried and tried at the office, but the words just wouldn't come. Not even the beginnings of a draft.

I'll just ignore it! Worked last time.

A comfortable setting and a few of his favorite things around him would relax him and allow the words to flow. It always paid to give close attention to the actions of daily living. A good way to distract that constant critical voice inside his head.

Anthony left work early, to prove to himself, once again, his treasured hypothesis, "The way to make sure you do something you hate is to make sure you laser-focus your attention on other things for a while."

He stopped by Top Pepe's to pick up his favorite chicken enchiladas with Christmas chile. *Best enchiladas in town!*

As he got home, he was greeted by the sight of the early winter sunset, glowing gold and pink over the Sandia Mountains through both the kitchen window and the French doors that led from the kitchen to the patio, a nightly show that he too often missed when he was at work. It made his beloved Sandias even more beautiful than usual. He put his tablet on the kitchen table, put the enchiladas in the refrigerator, then dug out some nice grapes to scatter on the patio, for the birds.

Anthony sat at the table across from the kitchen door, watching the house wrens with their little red-crested heads, as they realized that there'd be special treats for them all tonight.

Shouldn't they have flown south already?

His feathered guests were calling to each other as they pecked at Anthony's gift. Not singing, really. They only did that in summer. As night started to conquer day, Anthony began thinking of the nights he'd spent camping up in those mountains. Not just camping, but eating, too, by the light of a warm campfire.

He surveyed the contents of the crystal bowl (an inheritance from his mother) on the table in front of him. It was heaped high with ripe Comice pears. Promising himself he'd have one for dessert, he took the ripest, plumpest one and put it in the refrigerator. It was then that Anthony realized that watching the birds so enthusiastic about their food had made him hungry earlier than usual.

Anthony took the chicken enchiladas out of the refrigerator, grabbed a microwave safe plate, put them on it, covered it, set the microwave to heat them up, then sat, luxuriating, for almost the full three minutes in their chile-laden aroma.

Once the microwave's "it's going to be done soon" beep warned him, it took him less than thirty seconds to retrieve from the cupboard his favorite smooth china plate, the bright white one with the green border, its center hand-painted with bold red poppies. He enjoyed tracing with his fingers the brushstrokes as they sat atop the mirror-like china. Using his favorite plate as a charger, and savoring his memories of Henrietta, who'd given him the plates with the poppies, at least as much as the food itself, Anthony dawdled over dinner, watching the last of the sunlight vanish as he savored the taste and feel and aroma of every bite.

The pear had cooled off just enough now. He took it from the refrigerator to the sink to wash it, dried it and gently put it on what was now his smaller plate, also painted with brilliant red poppies.

By the time he'd gotten back to the table with his pear, he'd received an urgent message from his subconscious, telling him how to start the argument. *Score another one for 'my side!* Anthony exalted as he logged onto his tablet and started to work.

*****

Léonie Rosenstiel has won numerous awards for her work from SouthWest Writers and New Mexico Press Women. She has written, edited and contributed to more than dozen books. Her *Protecting Mama* reached Number one on Amazon's New Titles in Elder Abuse on December 11, 2021. The prequel is scheduled for publication this fall.

Second Place   **Ed Lehner**

Grantston

My cellphone light was getting dimmer. There had to be another way out. But these old mine usually had only one main shaft. It was cold and damp. The air was filled with dust. It was getting harder and harder to breath. The cellphone light went out. Pitch black.

I jerked awake, shaking, drenched with sweat. It was the same dream, every night. It was ten years now. I had to go back and try to find closure and maybe find peace.

*****

At 13,265 ft., Randall Mountain loomed over the town of Grantston, a small mountain town a little more than three hundred miles southwest of Denver in the San Juan Mountains. The town was named after Robert James Grant who owned and oversaw the Lucky Silver Mine which was about one-third up from the base of the mountain.

The mine had been shuttered now for over seventy years leaving the once vital town of 5000 people, during the mining heyday, suffering through years of declining population until the old narrow gauge railway that once hauled ore seventy miles south down to a smelter in the town of Santa Rita, was turned into a scenic railway for tourists. It was now a popular attraction for the many who came to ride it during the season from late April into October. The town's economy was now vibrant with the influx of summer tourists who rode the train or came to hike, mountain bike, and backpack into the surrounding wilderness. There were also music camps ranging from classical to folk and bluegrass, for children through adults.

Grantston was now busy through the summer from before Memorial Day until things began tapering off after Labor Day on into October when the aspen leaves had lit up the mountains with gold, faded and fallen to the ground.

Lucy Kramer, Karen Weber, Billy Gray, and I were best of friends, inseparable ever since grade school. That summer we had graduated from our small high school and were most likely spending our last time together. Lucy and I were heading off to college at the end of August, and Karen was going to cosmetology school in Denver. Only Billy was staying to work at his family's lumber and hardware store that had been in his family for three generations.

Karen and Lucy were tomboys, always game for whatever adventure we two boys wanted to go on. Billy was usually the planner of our adventures, always wanting to push us to our limits. He was a charismatic character, fun to be around but was a loose canon, having no boundaries when it came to the possibility of enjoying an adrenaline rush, such as racing down a treacherous mountain single track at breakneck speed on his mountain bike while the rest of us would tread much more carefully. Whatever it was, he liked living on the edge, like it was important that he live his life quickly.

We spent our high school summers with part time jobs and mountain biking or hiking in the back country, with Billy always in the lead.

That summer, we all felt a new sense of freedom and excitement with the realization we had no more high school and were going to be off to experience more of the world, heading toward adulthood. It was exhilarating, like doing a tricky descent down a single track with the elation never going away.

On the second Saturday of July we headed out into the early morning chill, which was quickly fading with the bright Colorado sun, into the mountains on our bikes. On our way out of town, Billy said, "I know what we should do. Let's go up to the old mine."

Karen said, "That's off limits, Billy. The road's closed off and there are 'No Trespassing' signs everywhere. That's a bad idea."

"Come on. That's from a long time ago. Nobody'll care. Nobody'll even know. It'll be fun. I heard there's lots of old mining shit up there."

"No, Billy. We shouldn't," I said. "You know the history."

"Exactly, it's just history, the operative word being history." He laughed as he turned, squeezed around the barriers and headed up the old unused road to the mine. We hesitated, looked at each other for approval, then reluctantly followed Billy for another adventure.

*****

Randall Mountain was a tomb containing the bodies of forty-nine miners, buried when the mine collapsed some seventy-five years ago. The shocked and outraged families and friends of the lost miners subsequently attacked the home of Robert James Grant, and burned it to the ground. Then they hung Robert James Grant from the neck in the town center until dead for his lack of safety concerns in the mine which everyone assumed to have been the cause of the tragic cave in. His body was buried in a shallow unmarked grave. The mine entrance was sealed off and had been closed ever since. The road was blocked and no one knew of anyone who had ever gone up there since.

Rumors floated about of strange happenings up there. Some claimed to have seen lights moving about. Others claimed to have heard bone chilling moans and cries that would turn one's blood to ice water.

My parents had warned me more than once to never ever go near that mine, but here I was, stupidly following Billy in direct disobedience of my parents, and I'm pretty sure we were breaking some sort of law. Lucy and Karen voiced their objections as well, but here we were, against our better judgement, following Billy to a place where we shouldn't be.

*****

We had climbed the rough rock strewn road to where it gratefully began to level off. We saw rusting pieces of machinery scattered about: old mining cars, a boiler, some sort of winch and other unknown things, even an old car. There were old mining structures, some heavy timbered and others that could have been housing or offices.

My heart was racing, not only from the climb on my bike, but from nervousness of being there. I didn't like the way it felt, like some evil place, feeling dangerous, foreboding, like we were disturbing something best left undisturbed. I was startled by a sharp pop from behind me.

"Hey Trevor, my front tire just blew," Karen yelled.

"I've got a spare tube," I said.

"Yeah. I've got one too. Help me change it?"

"Sure," I said as I sat down on a rock to get my breath and drink some water and waited for her and Lucy.

Billy yelled to us from a hundred yards away, "Hey. Come on you guys. Let's go in. There's nothing but old rotted boards over the entrance, it'll be easy."

I yelled back, "We're fixing Karen's flat tire and we're not going in there and neither should you. You stay out of there. It's dangerous."

"Naaah. I want to see what's in there. Maybe I'll find a silver nugget," he yelled back. "Wait for me."

The tire had a new tube, was on the bike and aired up. We were about to go to call for Billy when we felt the ground shake. Then we saw the explosion of dust and debris blast out of the opening of the mine, then heard the rumbling like the whole mountain was collapsing around us. We all stood, frozen in place by fear. Once the shaking subsided we saw through the dust that one of the heavy structures by the mine entrance was now just a pile of debris. We looked at each other with our eyes bulging out of our heads with fear. In unison we screamed, "Billy."

After the incident, things got really ugly in Grantston for the three of us. We were blamed for letting Billy go into the mine, even accused of daring him to do so. We and our families had become pariahs. I was let go from my job. My summer was over and I left early for college. Later that year, my family left and moved to Los Lunas, New Mexico.

*****

It was as if I had never been in Granston before, as I once again walked Main Street. It was a different town. A few stores and restaurants were the same as I remembered but many had changed hands and were now different. The music camps were still going. And there was a new gentrification that had lost much of the western mining mountain town atmosphere of when I was growing up. Billy's parents had sold the old family business and moved to Arizona. As I walked around town I didn't recognize anyone. Then I saw a woman that looked like Karen walking towards me. It was Karen. She had matured into a beautiful woman, her long black hair, tanned features and toned body made me stare. Hopefully my mouth wasn't open.

Then she saw me and almost ran to me. "Oh-my-god, Trevor Johnson. What the hell are you doing back here? I haven't seen or heard from you in like forever. How are you?" she said with a welcoming smile.

"Hi Karen," I said trying to act normal and not like a stupid teenager. "I . . . I'm doing great. I had no idea you were here. Do you live here?"

"Yeah, I moved back a few years ago. I went to cosmetology school and worked in Denver afterwards, but got tired of traffic and the big city in general, moved back and started my own hair salon and here I am. The place has changed. So much new blood. Hey, got time. I just closed for the day. Let's go get a drink and catch up."

"Sure. I'd like that. Lead the way."

She took me to what used to be an old tavern that was now restored and upgraded but still maintained some of the rustic charm of old. We found a table by the large window in front for the light and people watching on the sidewalk.

We ordered, Karen a glass of chardonnay, me, a beer. She led off, "So, Trevor, what've you been doing? Where are you living? Why are you back here?"

"Well, I work for a small tech firm in Albuquerque." Then I told her of why I needed to return for a visit. "I still miss him, Karen. I don't think there's a day that goes by that I don't think of him. I need closure . . . or something."

She looked at me with sad eyes. "I know. Maybe that's one of the reasons I came back, to face the reality. I often think of him too. I don't know if you know, but the town finally came to grips with that mine after Billy's death. Engineers determined that the shaft was now completely sealed by the cave-in so it is now open to the public and is like a memorial. I can take you up there tomorrow if you'd like."

I hesitated, "I'm not sure I can. But I guess I should. Maybe that's why I'm here." We were finishing our drinks, "Want another wine?"

"Not here. Let's go and have dinner. And we can talk some more."

"Sounds good. I am getting hungry. Where to?"

"Follow me'" she said.

I threw some cash on the table for the drinks and we left for a new restaurant that advertised a "true mountain menu". Unlike the description of some special sort of "mountain menu", the food was good basic American fare available in any town or city. We ate and chatted for over an hour and a half. The waiter brought our check and stood, waiting for us to pay.

"I think they want our table. Let's go to my place and continue. It's only a few blocks away."

We paid and walked in the alpenglow of the early evening. The mountains to the east were lit with the setting sun that still hit the tops of the peaks. The high altitude chill was setting in with the warmth of the sun gone for another day.

Karen's house was a remodeled, cozy one-time miner's home. She showed me into the living room, gently furnished with a comfortable looking couch and matching chair, some artwork prints on the wall, and flowers on the small dining table. She motioned me towards the couch, then lit some candles which gave the room an even warmer feeling. She opened a bottle of wine, poured us each a glass and came and sat beside me, close beside me. We continued our conversation from the restaurant, trying to avoid any mention of Billy.

We were on our second glass of wine when she reached to me and kissed me, first warm and gentle, then she put her hands around my neck and deepened her kiss. I returned her kiss, not sure about what was happening.

She broke away and sat back, "I'm sorry. I shouldn't have done that. But . . . I've wanted to ever since we were kids. I had such a crush on you back during high school, but Lucy was in my way. She wanted you, and I stood aside. But you just ignored her blatant flirting. Then, well then, we know what happened and it all changed for us. When I saw you today all those feelings I had for you came back."

She looked at me, expecting something back and I tried to sort out the thoughts rolling through my head, quickly going back to that summer and I remembered changing her tire and how she looked at me and gave unneeded touches while pretending to help. I remember feeling something then, more than just friendship. But then, Billy.

"Trevor, are you okay? Say something."

"I . . . I was just remembering something, changing your tire And how I felt something different for you. I'm feeling really stupid right now. I'm sorry I'm not responding better but —."

"It's okay. I understand. But I've waited too long." She smiled, got up, took my hand and led me to her bedroom.

The morning sun shone bright, right into my eyes, blurring me awake. Karen was already up and entered the room a moment later.

"Com'n and get dressed. We'll grab coffee and a breakfast sandwich at one of the food trucks."

"Where are we going?" I asked as I was going into the bathroom.

"Up to the mine."

We headed down to main street and Karen asked, "Where are you staying?"

"At the old hotel."

"We'll stop so you can get your stuff and check out. You'll stay with me while you're here. I can at least have you that long."

We got our food and Karen headed her Jeep out of town towards the mountain. "Lucy and I still make contact at Christmas, first cards and now an email," she said. She married some guy from college and lives out in the Bay Area. She's got two kids and seems happy."

I was too filled with anxiety to say anything in reply.

She turned up the road to the old mine. The road had been cleared of the big rocks and, while still rough, was fine riding in her Jeep. The old mining machinery was still there as I remembered, the old wooden structures still there. Apprehension was building heavy in my gut and I was wishing I hadn't eaten that breakfast burrito. She pulled into a new parking area. When got out of the Jeep, Karen took my hand and led me toward the mine. The path was lined with signage explaining the mine and its history.

Everything from ten years ago came rushing back. I wanted to leave but Karen steadfastly held on, dragging me to where the mine entrance once was. Then I saw the large granite memorial with the names of the forty-nine miners who died in the cave-in in 1939. Then I saw a smaller version of the memorial which read, "William (Billy) Joseph Gray, 1990-2008." Embedded in the top of the granite was a sliver nugget.

Randall Mountain loomed over us, soaring 13,265 ft. into a bright blue Colorado sky, like it was exerting its force, wanting respect. I was overwhelmed with memories, of our friendship, of that summer cut short. The two memorials stared at me in my too long repressed grieving. Was it complete? Was Randall satisfied now that it contained the souls of fifty men? Were those souls a sacrifice, payment for the intrusion into its bowels for its treasure? Was it fifty souls for thirty pieces of silver?"

Tears were running down my cheeks. Karen squeezed my hand and laid her head on my shoulder. "Are you okay?"

"No," I stammered out through the lump in my throat. "I should've stopped him, should've never followed him. Maybe he'd still be here."

"I know. We're all guilty of not trying to stop him. But we didn't. And it is what it is. I guess moving back here has helped me to dampen my own guilt. We have to let it go, Trevor."

"I know, I know. It's hard. Thanks for bringing me up here. It's good to be here. I think I may have finally, at last, come home." I felt a slight smile emerge from my tears. "I see Billy got his silver nugget."

*****

Retired professor, **Ed Lehner,** is a luthier, amateur musician, and enjoys writing poetry and fiction. He has written two novels and most recently published an anthology of short stories, ***Grandpa's Horse and Other Tales.*** You'll find more at his website, elehner.com. He hangs out with his wife, Julie, and their cat, Emma, in Southwest Colorado.

Third Place   **Mary Burns**

Mountain Meditation

Thoughts flit about my mind like the tiny motes in the sunlight as I walk along the forest path. I'm going to give up trying to focus. I should let go and be in the moment for now. I'll work out my plans somehow, sometime. I tell myself to let go of my imagined scenes of her car accident, the drama, and the chaos long over. The lights fade and the curtain falls on that scene.

A mile in and I've left the scrub and junipers behind me and the air is cooler under the pines. My eye catches the color dabs in the growth beside the trail. LYFs, little yellow flowers, are still poking up even though the summer is near its end. The pine smell lifts my spirit and the breeze not only caresses and cools me but plays a soft song in the leaves above me as the small green and yellow forms dance in the sunlight. A cloud of no-see-ums floats in a sun shaft in front of me and I circle the troublesome patch. Sandy ground has transformed to brown earth shot with tree roots and mixed with bits of rock and brown leaves. My sticks keep me steady as the trail winds downward for a brief spell, then switches back and upward again.

It's still early and there is plenty of daylight left for this hike. The forest is quiet with an occasional bird call, but little sign of other life. A soft rustle in the bushes to my left. Something small and wary of an encounter. I'm no threat and I smile at the very idea.

No signs of any larger life. Perhaps I'll see a deer in the distance, but so far nothing. The larger animals are here I know. Fox, bobcat, bear, and mountain lion remain in their hidden homes. I feel their presence as this is their world, but I'll not likely see them. Bears. Yes, there have been numerous encounters with bears over the years, but not in these woods. I have had bear encounters in the old Appalachian ranges, and in other Western mountains too. A bit scary of course, but always a positive outcome. I've come to believe that the bear is my spirit animal after so many meetings, and it's a very comforting thought.

Another turn in the path as I round a rock protrusion and an opening in the trees presents a view of distant mountains against a vivid blue sky. Several ranges in the distance appear less distinct and smokey, one beyond the other. Another outcropping of rock provides a seat in the sun. I'm soothed by the view and the breezes have intensified here and are keeping the heat from the sun under control. A drink of water to refresh and a chance to catch my breath and slow down my heart rate. The elevation is tiring and I need to take these stops more often than I like.

Disconnected from the world, but what? My phone vibrates. I am not taking this call. Good grief, is there no escape? I shut my phone off completely and stash it in my pack. Awakened so rudely from the immersion in my surroundings that I was basking in, I come face to face with the dilemma I have been dodging. No, I'm just not ready to take on this argument again. I've been over the pros and cons several times. The curse of the analytic. Why can't I just go with my gut feelings? But I don't trust my heart when I think that it is overly influenced by fear.

OK, time to continue the hike and follow this path to its conclusion, even if my own path is left uncertain. A downward scramble into a canyon leaves my knees a bit wobbly as I skid on a gravelly path entering the clearing that I sought. The slide makes me catch my breath and my heart is racing from the momentary fear of falling. Rocky cliffs cast shadows over most of the floor before me, but sunlight catches a small waterfall in the near distance. It is not much more than a trickle, but a pleasant surprise. Just runoff from last night's rain, but unexpected.

I shed my pack and dig around for my sandwich and settle down on a fallen tree to enjoy my lunch. The beauty of the day and this mountain haven lift my spirits. The quiet soothes the last of my stress away and, settling further, I watch as a squirrel ventures into the space and drinks from the water at the base of the falls.

Thoughts bubble up despite my every attempt to just zone out in the moment. Perhaps it is time to face my future and determine where I am going. Okay, what am I so afraid of that I can't make this decision? Is it fear of change itself? We all have times of change that we have to face. This crossroad is timely as my work here is done. The project was completed with success and I have money saved. Many of the friends I've made here are scattering and moving on to other places. But I've fallen in love with this place. My heart feels a connection here as it has in no other place I've been.

But my family needs me. I know that it will only be for a few months until she recovers and is back on her feet. I can decide what comes next for me while I help out. I won't be locked into this move. But I know that this isn't the first time that this has happened and it probably won't be the last. I take a deep breath and wish it were not so. I really don't want to deal with this, but I can't always do what I want. I fear getting sucked into the emotional traps that surely await me. The twisted logic and mental games and circular arguments that can never be resolved.

I close my eyes and breathe deeply for several minutes feeling my heart slow and letting my body relax. Taking the next step, I clear my mind and cast my thoughts out into space to connect with the greater consciousness. I feel the lift in my head as I reach out for answers. I love the feeling of opening my heart and mind. The top of my head feels like it is expanding and moving outward as I focus on the steady soft sound of water trickling over the rocks. I drift for some time as I continue to breathe deeply inhaling the clean air and clearing my thoughts. I sit still for an unmeasurable length of time waiting for the knowledge I am sure will come. A deeper quiet enfolds me and I become aware that I am no longer alone. I open my eyes but see no one. Closing my eyes again I see light through my eyelids and hear a voice. The trickling water playing over the canyon cliff is telling me a tale.

"You are free and you can go. Don't be afraid. You are strong and stable as these mountain rocks and yet you are also as free as these mountain winds. You carry us with you in your heart and mind. You can touch us anytime that you wish. Just close your eyes and open your heart and mind. We will be here waiting for your return."

My eyes open wide and the sunlight shimmers. An epiphany! Joy fills me! The ancient spirit of the mountain that I love has touched me. A blessing and a promise to keep connected with me no matter what I do or where I go. The anxiety of the unresolved has vanished and I am calm in my knowledge of what I should do. Yes, I will take up the challenge of her care, but with an open heart and positive intention. There will be time for my plans when I return. The path may take me in directions that I hadn't planned to go, but I trust that it is where I am supposed to be.

The shadows are growing and the breeze carries a cooler feel as I pack up. I notice a rock shaped like a bear fetish and marvel as it shimmers in the last of the sun. I tuck it into my pocket. A mountain gift smoothed by waters, wind, and sand over time. With a newfound strength I look about and my mind captures the moment. The trail continues with a short loop back to the main path and I return home and make my plans.

*****

Mary Burns recently retired to New Mexico after her career as a successful insurance executive. An avid reader, she dreamed of one day having time to create her own stories. The Land of Enchantment cast its spell and she is now writing short stories, memoirs, and the beginnings of several novels.

Looking for Company

Photo Submitted by Robert Cudney

Section Eleven

Prose – Celestial Bodies

When we designated Celestial Bodies as a category we had no idea what direction the stories would travel. Would it be a space story, an angel, or a really beautiful person?

Two of the three best stories of this group were in the realm of science fiction/fantasy. The most moving one, however, was an introspective.

First Place   **Angel Salvador Chiuteña**

Orion

I can recognize three prominent dots. The rest, just scattered night sky sparkles. I force my brain to try harder. It makes out a diamond pendant, an unidentified flying object, a crystal ball. At one point, one star appears to be a car with its high beams racing into the night.

But a Greek hunter with a shield would be a bit of a stretch.

"That's his shield, and there, his shoulders. Do you see it?", he asks.

"Uh-huh," I whisper.

I don't. I brush his arm though, while his finger connects the shimmering dots. Something about my brain doesn't connect A to B to B to C without being distracted by a.1 to a.10, b.1 to b.10, and so on. I play some music on my phone to accompany him while I drift into the misty darkness. Now, the car transforms into a firefly flying circles around a silver rose.

*****

You are 30 years old, three decades of leaving footprints in this ever-changing land. It feels like a hundred years to you. It is a blink of an eye for me.

Your heart whispers, "It is a beautiful sky. That's all you need to know". But your mind refuses to believe that things can be effortlessly beautiful. There must be a backstory, a galactic explosion, an accidental collision, a tragic reason. There should be ugly before beauty. There should be sorrow before joy.

There is beauty in this world, above and below you, surrounding you. I've cradled earthquakes and birthed mountains. Believe me when I say, when a miracle flashes before you, it's better to accept it than to understand.

*****

"Third one!" he exclaims. "This is the most shooting star I've seen in my whole life."

"Did you wish?", I ask.

"Of course."

I did too. That's how I know the superstitions aren't true, because if they are, his lips would trace constellations on mine right now.

The fourth one reminds me of another myth. Shooting stars are souls escaping purgatory, allowing them to finally begin the ascent to heaven and peace.

And that's how I know the myth is a lie, because if it isn't, I'm sure I would not be left here without a goodbye.

I don't know what to do with all these stars.

*****

I'm not even holding a shield. I don't have a belt. I'm not an eagle, or a ram. I am neither the stars nor the sky. Although you can believe that if you wish. Up above is just as deep as down below. I know how drowning it is to be in the middle of it all, so use what you can from me. When my tears light across the night sky before burning out into a point of inky blackness, close your eyes and make a wish, if that will bring your soul some peace.

*****

I wish my eyes could capture a moment for what it truly is, the view, the feeling, the story. Cameras just don't give it justice.

I let him try though, he's good at it. He will photograph just enough memories to look back when he feels like it. He will capture it with his eyes, like he captured me.

I try to focus on the sky again. Fuck it, I can't see the hunter. But it's still beautiful. Please, please, just focus on it being beautiful. I just wish there's proof that something is up there, that there is a reason I'm here, watching dead stars still shining, holding a man that has mastered leaving.

*****

Look down. I'm not above, well, not only above. I'm at the monuments, still standing. I'm with the wind blowing. I'm in the stars falling. I'm in your chest, beating. I'm with that man's hand you're holding. Listen. Millions of years and trillions of stars, yet there are still no answers. You are broken and full, questioning and learning. You are burning to ashes and rising from pieces. You are doing it right.

*****

"Hey! You made a friend!" he yells. I stand up and find a cat sneaking under my hammock. His green eyes shatter the darkness.

I guess this is the hunter I've been looking for.

"Hi Orion."

*****

Angel Salvador Chiuteña is the author of *Whispering Mementos*, a poetry and short story collection. She aspires to showcase her culture as a Filipino through poetry and short stories. She had won several writing awards for flash fiction and creative nonfiction.

Second Place   **Kathleen Holmes**

The Music Box

A crack of light appears in the sky every time a dead musician gets dropped into the box. The light is bright white and can be easily missed if you're not looking up. A zen gong player who lives a few doors down told me the musicians who disappear without a trace have actually gone to be reborn. That would explain shifts in population. They do come and go.

One song ends as another begins. When I'm in the mood to play my jazz trombone, I blow before someone else can start their song. It took a lot of practice to get my lips in the door around town.

The entire city infrastructure is made from pieces of broken instruments; guitar strings are strung for suspension bridges. Whole buildings are made from xylophone keys. Every structure is an architectural marvel. I've been working on a filagree design in my apartment window from a bag of violin tuning hardware—you know, those nuts around the tuning pegs that look like tiny gears and washers.

There's an endless supply of new and broken instruments everywhere I go and, believe me, I have walked the entire length of this square box; north, south, east and west. We either shrink once we pass into the white light zone or this box is huge, although I'm not sure what I can compare it to.

It's been decades since anyone tried to open the lid. The last man who climbed up there was an oboe player. He was strong and athletic. All eyes had watched while he pushed on the lid as hard as he could. Whether he moved it at all is highly debatable and can lead to arguments. Sad song musicians believe it's impossible for dead spirits to lift the lid from inside. Creators of happy music believe anything is possible. Most of us jazz musicians don't care.

Nonetheless, the oboe player, who achieved greater fame in death than in life, pushed so hard he fell from his makeshift scaffolding and disappeared on the way down.

Another controversial subject discussed in polite I society is, 'WHO poked the holes in the top of our box?' I know—it sounds funny, huh? Sitting around small tables with no need for food or drink. I don't care who poked the holes in the lid of the box. Isn't it a greater mystery that we are all stuck inside this box after we die, caput, not so gone?

We know the box is made from an excellent grade of recycled cardboard to have held up through the ages. Even the sharpest bit, forged from the screws of a bassoon, can't penetrate the walls of this box.

Someone who loves music must have punched the holes in the lid so our sounds could leak out for others to hear. The twinkling shafts of light are soothing and inspire a LOT of music. Don't get me started. The list of songs written about beams of light is endless.

I ran into Amy Winehouse at the library while ago. The shelves are filled with printed music; that's all we have to read here. Amy asked if I'd heard about the town meeting at Woodwind Hill tomorrow. She always knows what's going on. According to Amy her death was a huge wake up call. Anyway—there goes Janice Joplin again. I wish she'd learn to sing. I'd rather listen to Etta James any day. Where was I? Oh yeah, the meeting.

Elite classical musicians throughout the ages have held political sway as long as anyone here can remember. Most of us could care less about being in control of the box. Wars and clashes over genres of music use to take up a lot of time until residents decided to expand their musical appreciation. It got kind of dicey during the sixties when rock and roll musicians started dropping with unprecedented numbers into the box.

Life is better now. It's no big deal to see Jimi Hendrix accompanying Mozart on piano. They've worked out a lot of stuff.

I don't think I'll go to the meeting tomorrow. It's always nice to see the shine on Luciano Pavarotti's patent leather shoes but nothing ever gets solved and we don't need more rules. If I stay home it will give me a chance to practice my trombone. I can't wait to finish the window. The filigree's going to look like lace. I like it here.

*****

Kathleen Holmes is a resident of Aztec, NM. She has written feature articles for *The Anvil's Ring* – a magazine for the Artist Blacksmith Association of North America, and short stories in *The New Settler Interview*. In 2021 *A New Mexico Love Story* appeared in the SWW anthology: *Ramblings & Reflections*.

Third Place   **Roger Floyd**

The Star Falls

An uninhabited planet, tiny, unobtrusive, beyond the resolution of Earth's telescopes. Wild and beautiful in its own minimalistic way, with broad expansive deserts that stretch endlessly beyond the horizon, interrupted here and there by towering escarpments that rise abruptly from the sand like broad curtains of bronze and umber. Almost devoid of plant life, limited to diminutive specimens with narrow greenish-gray leaves, growing from the sand only near water which they find either on the surface or underground, harbingers of oases in an otherwise deserted landscape. Occasional small lakes of turquoise blue and emerald green, huddled near mountains that soar into the stratosphere, well above the broad, flat plains that surround them. Fed by small streams that drain from the mountains and merge into creeks and brooks that, on Earth, the largest of which would barely qualify for a name.

We journeyed there, Sue and I—Sue the astronomer, I the naturalist—the first visitors from Earth to this unique world, sent to study the heavens from the point of view of this planet. The planet orbits a small sun, warm and brilliant, but only about half the size of Earth's sun. Barely enough to give sustenance to the plant life. Nights are cool and breezy, but days are warm. A perfect environment for a young couple like us, just learning how to travel through outer space, but willing to take a risk to visit an unknown world as explorers *nouveau*, making our way in the burgeoning field of planetary exploration.

But, as with all voyages, dangers exist. The sun of this planet is a companion to a red giant star, Betelgeuse, known for many centuries to be in the late stages of expansion. A dangerous star, ready to go supernova at any moment. As a huge pulsating mass of solar protoplasm, galactic mariners for years have felt strange emanations from that star. So often, when they ventured too close to it, or tried to go into orbit around it, problems occurred in their spacecraft and many times they lost control over it. We have heard of spacecraft drifting into the outer atmosphere of the star, unable to resist the pull, destroyed by the intense heat, all hands lost. They named it the Red Menace, and even today interstellar ships give it a wide berth. It's in its last days as a cohesive body and soon will collapse in on itself in a supernova explosion.

Only light hours away, Betelgeuse dominates our sky, especially at night, but it can be seen even in daytime. Bulging and spitting, it sends showers of subatomic particles into space on an aggravatingly irregular basis. We shield ourselves from those showers that come our way, and we have grown used to having to leave our tent and duck into the shield house at all hours of the day or night. On those occasions when the ejections last for several hours, we have even had to sleep in the shield house.

Yet, there is a fascination we have developed with Betelgeuse, Sue especially. It intrigues us, it captivates us, and we can't look away.

Both Sue and I felt the red star's presence almost as soon as we landed, Sue more strongly than I. Many nights I would find her outside staring at it, lost in its emanations, transfixed by its weak light. Sometimes I have had to lead her to the shield house by the hand, to break the spell it seems to have cast over her. After the star dips below the horizon, she wakes from her spell and apologizes for being intoxicated by the star's hold, but I never know if her explanation is real or merely exigent. I try to get her to talk about it, but she is hesitant to speak. Frequently she replies with a simple, "I can't look away."

Meanwhile, we continue to explore the planet. Or what little we can reach on foot. We cannot go far; we have to remain close to the shield house in case the star throws particles our way. But in our limited forays, we have found wild plants that produce edible fruits and vegetables which we have learned to cook and prepare to our own delight. Twice, in every yearly rotation of our planet around its central star, Betelgeuse disappears behind our sun for several days, and we are able to explore much farther away from our main camp site. We have also been able to take our tent down and move the camp to other sites, towing the shield house behind us because it is on wheels and we have a mobile power unit.

But Sue's fascination with Betelgeuse grows more and more troubling. Often she spends hours just staring at the star, lost in all faculties, difficult to break into. Only when I place a blindfold across her eyes have I been able to get her to return to the tent or dart to the shield house.

More and more often she remains in the trance-like state the star holds over her.

When we first arrived, Betelgeuse was prominent in the night sky, but as our planet orbits its own star, Betelgeuse soon became visible in the day time. Each morning it rises earlier and earlier, in infinitesimal increments, greeting us as we rise to begin our day.

I do not know what attraction Sue feels for the star. I must confess I am attracted to it myself, but in a milder way than Sue. The star has a calming effect on me, perhaps that's true on any observer. Yet Sue's infatuation is more than just calming. In what little she has said about the star, she insists it calls her to visit. Such a situation, of course, I cannot understand.

Now that Betelgeuse is in the daylight sky, we have difficulty getting any work done. Plant life needs examining, rocks have to be collected and cataloged, images of the terrain must be taken and maps prepared, water should be collected and purified for consumption. Our day is full of necessary tasks. Yet Sue spends so much time staring at the star, her attention riveted and her eyes glazed over, that many tasks go unfinished. "I have visited it," she says. I mock her. She responds with a mere shrug.

One evening, alone in our tent, with Betelgeuse on the other side of the planet, she begins to talk about the star.

"They've come to me. I knew they would. I talk to them. Not verbally, of course, but I have conversed with them. They've invited me to visit. To become a part of them. To become a part of the star. I will visit again tomorrow."

"Who's 'they'?" I ask, but she replies with a shrug. I do not know how to take what she says, and I am left with the feeling that she believes everything she has told me since we arrived, now almost a half-year later.

The next day, as the sun rises and warms the air at our camp, she leaves the tent. Betelgeuse has yet to make its appearance. I begin to take images of our camp site, starting with broad, wide-angle photos of the terrain all around, with Sue in some of the pictures for reference. Later, I focus on an interesting formation of rocks at the base of a waterfall cascading off a steep rock wall more than fifty meters high. The fall is so high much of the water never makes it to the pool below, whipped into vapor as it descends in the lower gravity of this planet. Most of the vapor is carried away on the breeze that swirls about the falls.

But Betelgeuse soon rises above the horizon in the east and Sue has halted all her work. She stands transfixed by the star, staring at it out beyond the vast desert that stretches away from the escarpment. Behind me the waterfall continues to hiss, a doleful sound, melancholy, as if portending a serious incident. As I watch, she begins to fade from my view. She becomes transparent, and I can see through her. Eventually she disappears altogether. I run to where she stood, yelling her name. I look all around, I scan the entire area, from the campsite to the escarpment and the waterfall. My mind falters—*Where is she? Where is she?* Panicky, I yell her name over and over, swiveling my head from one side to the other, frantically looking for her. Behind me the waterfall continues its hiss, saying ". . . she's gone . . . she's gone . . ."

Yet, in what I realized later was only about ten seconds of real time but what seemed hours as it occurred, she reappears, in the same spot she stood before, seemingly the same as when she disappeared, with little outward sign of anything happening.

"Sue!" I yell. "Are you okay? What happened? Where did you go?" I pummel her with questions, but she barely acknowledges my presence. She turns and enters the tent and lies down on her sleeping bag. I continue to press her for an explanation.

"I visited the star," she says slowly and quietly. "It was lovely."

"What do you mean you visited it? How can you visit a star? Where did you go? What did you do? Do you know you disappeared?"

"Yes, I know. They took me. To the star, to the inside of the star. There is so much to see."

"To see? To *see*? What can you see inside a star? Were you in a spaceship or something? A spacesuit that can resist the heat inside a star? I don't understand."

"Please, leave me alone. I'm tired from my trip. I need to rest."

"How can you be tired? You were gone for only a few seconds."

"It seemed like days. I was gone for many days. I lost count. It was a very tiring trip. We saw so many things."

"We? Who's we? I don't understand—"

"Please, leave me alone. I have to rest."

I leave her alone in the tent and she seems to fall asleep after I step outside. But I cannot work; question after question pollutes my brain and I cannot concentrate on any real task. I pace the area, trying to make sense of the incident. I visit the site on which she stood when she disappeared and gaze at the star. I feel a warm glow from the star as I have so many times before, but even though I stare at it for many minutes, I gain no further insight into how she could have disappeared. It does not talk to me as it does to Sue. I pick up a plastic pail and gather water from the pool. As I pour it through the sterilizing filter, the waterfall still hisses at me, ". . . she's gone . . . she's gone . . ."

Daybreak comes all too soon, and Sue is up, refreshed from her journey the previous day. We have a small first meal and begin to work. But soon Betelgeuse rises above the horizon and Sue is entranced again. I stay with her, never moving more than one meter away. At first she ignores the star, but abruptly she turns her head and stares at it, listening to an unseen and unheard voice.

"What?" she says, gently, inquisitively, as though answering a child's call. "I'll be there."

She walks back to the spot where she disappeared the day before. I walk with her and put my arms around her. She does not resist, yet again she turns transparent and eventually is gone, out of my grasp. I cannot hold her tightly enough.

As the day before, she returns a few seconds later, exactly where she was, within my embrace. I hold her, I support her as she almost faints and we walk back to the tent where she lies down on her sleeping bag.

"I'm so tired," she says. "We went everywhere. We saw everything. It was wonderful."

"We?" I ask. "Who's 'we'?"

"It's hard to describe. The ones who took me . . ."

She remains on her sleeping bag for the rest of the day and into the night. Outside the tent the waterfall continues to hiss its ominous sound. A warning, perhaps?

The next morning, before Betelgeuse rises, and during a short breakfast, Sue begins to tell me about her last trip. She speaks of stars of red and blue and yellow and gold, of nebula and galaxies, seen from afar and from within, star clusters with birthing stars exploding in vibrant colors as the first fusions of hydrogen nuclei occur within their cores. She tells of planets of molten rock where diamonds fall from the sky, and where life forms of extravagant sizes and shapes wander through jungles of ice and snow and oddly-shaped plants of green and brown and maroon and orange. I cannot keep up with her descriptions, she rattles them off so fast. I am impressed with her travels, but a little jealous too—why wasn't I included in her trips? Is it because she is the astronomer of our little group? Has some supernatural intelligence selected her because they knew she'd be able to understand what they showed her? My brain won't wrap around all the information.

Now Betelgeuse appears and Sue, slowly at first, works her way over to the spot where the disappearances occurred. She stands there for a moment, and in another moment is gone. I watch, still fascinated, yet scared and concerned for her safety. She reappears only a few seconds after she left, yet her descriptions of what she saw and did could only have taken place over several months, if not a year. A year in a few seconds? I cannot understand, and I do not even try.

Every day the same thing occurs. She disappears, for only a few seconds, yet she has days and months of stories to tell. Sometimes I try to hold her, other times I let her go and watch from a distance. Four times it happens—five times, six times, then seven and eight.

Nine times. The tenth time approaches.

On the tenth time I stand beside her, not embracing her, only holding her hand. She stares at the star, a look of peace on her face, a slight smile, the anticipation of another voyage to places of magnificent beauty and fascination. Shortly before she begins to disappear, she turns to me and says, "I will see you later. Don't wait for me." Then she disappears.

"What?" I say. "Where? What did you mean?"

She does not reappear as usual a few seconds later. I step away from the site. I look for her, but with her admonition ringing in my ears, I retreat to the tent. She never reappears on the surface of this planet.

\#

I have begun the arduous year-long voyage back to Earth. After a half-year since her disappearance, Sue has failed to materialize, and I have become unable to continue this project alone. I have asked to be relieved.

The latest high-speed space drives have taken me in forty-five Earth days to a planet about one light-month from Betelgeuse, still within the red star's sphere of influence, but far enough away that the emanations are no longer dangerous. I have landed in a small shuttlecraft at a spaceport on this planet, and from here I will transfer to the intragalactic excursion to the vicinity of Earth, and, finally, home. In the night sky, the big red star still throbs and spits, like a bully trying to exert some control over all it surveys, but forced to yield to the reality that spaceflight can still take people away from it. As I exit the shuttle I glance up at it. It holds no peril for me.

As I walk along the concourse from the shuttle toward the main passenger terminal, I gaze absentmindedly toward the building, and standing outside the door, waiting for me, is Sue, exactly as I saw her the day she left the little desert planet. I run to her and we embrace.

"How did you get here?" I ask.

"They dropped me here just before you arrived. I told them I wanted to see you again. I've seen so many things I could never have seen any other way. I'll tell you all about them, about who they are and why they took me, but later. We have so much catching up to do."

We embrace again and share a long, passionate kiss. But we are startled by a commotion, sharp gasps and shouts as others on the concourse look toward the sky and point upward.

"Look!" they say. "It's started."

I glance also, over Sue's shoulder, and the big red star has become much brighter. It swells and expands, sending incandescent hot gasses outward in the typical manner of a supernova explosion. Brighter and brighter it becomes, its light obscuring other stars nearby. People are yelling and screaming—panic has consumed the concourse. Sue turns and looks and cries out.

"Oh, no! It can't be. They told me that wouldn't happen for a long time. They promised! They said— No! No! It can't happen now! Not now. Not now. I'm not ready to go—"

"What is it?" I say, "Go where?" But Sue cannot speak, she is frozen in mid-scream. She turns transparent and disappears. I wait as I had before. Minutes go by—ten, twenty, thirty—but she does not reappear and I am left alone, my shadow cast eerily across the now empty concourse by the light from the expanding star.

*****

Roger Floyd is a retired PhD medical researcher who is now committed to writing science fiction and literary short stories full time. He has completed a trilogy of science fiction novels which are in various stages of preparation for self-publication. He also writes a blog about science, writing, and the environment at rogerfloyd.wordpress.com.

A Diversity of Expression

Section Twelve

Non-Fiction– Travel

If you want to visit somewhere you have never been, it is smart to have insights into what to expect. Travel reporters make a good living by taking down information and details of locations which others may want to visit someday and selling that information to magazines.

Readers want travel articles to provide insights over and above the base statistics they can find in any travel guide, as you will see in the following three pieces.

A Diversity of Expression

Wildly Shining

Photo submitted by Elizabeth S. Layton

First Place   **Connie Orozco-Morgan**

Of Titans and Sprites and Forest Delights

It is a folly to consider California as existing only between Los Angeles and San Francisco. North from the bay to the border with Oregon, for example, covers more than three hundred fifty miles and takes nearly seven hours. The most traveled path is Interstate 5 but the better choice takes longer and satisfies far more.

The trip on Highway 101 north of the bay is in order: the finery, the winery, the piney and the briny. The riches of San Rafael lead to the vineyards of Napa; they in turn become the forests of Mendocino and Humboldt before revealing the ocean views from Eureka to Crescent City. The drive is in itself a surreal trip even without any local chemical or natural enhancement. There is a time continuum north of Petaluma that slows everything down. In wine country, dozens of vineyards and tasting rooms vie for tastebuds and credit cards. Passing through Ukiah, the quaint farms and grape-laden hillsides fade and are replaced by trees, refreshing and cooling shade after the sunlit fields. Then the trees themselves change from deciduous to ever green, from short and round to tall and then taller.

The redwoods, *sequoia sempervirens,* are at first scattered amongst the sugar and ponderosa pines but soon dominate the view. But the real reward is at the heart of the mystical redwoods, where trees seem to be from another place and time. This is Longfellow's forest primeval "with garments green...and voices sad and prophetic." The highway at once cuts a swath through and respectfully curves around these titans as a visitor delves deeper and deeper.

The sun is now gone even on a mid-summers' day and the world becomes an emerald shell, quiet and comforting. The affect is universal. John Steinbeck said, "The most irreverent of men, in the presence of redwoods, goes under a spell of wonder and respect." Remain on the state highway and the forest alternates between sunlight

227

and shadow and the view of redwoods is impressive. But a driver with a little more time who opts for the bypass through Humboldt Redwoods State Park will be richly rewarded. The park is open twenty-four hours a day year-round and there is no fee to enter, so the choice is easy to make.

The Avenue of the Giants, a thirty-five mile scenic byway, winds like the snake around the staff of Asclepius, over and under and in parallel with Highway 101 from Garberville to Pepperwood. The forest on the highway is impressive enough but once on the Avenue, a driver is enveloped in green. The color isn't just evergreen; the filtered light and kaleidoscope layering combine to make kelly, lime and hunter but also chartreuse and viridian. The trees stretch toward the sky and there is a reverential feeling of being in a natural cathedral. Deeply creviced and fibrous bark enrobe massive trunks some more than thirty feet in diameter.

Branches begin fifty to one hundred feet above the ground. The trunks are not so much brown as burnt umber and cinnamon. Bulbous outgrowths or burls, typically near the ground but sometimes ten feet up are the nesting eggs of future redwoods, waiting for fire or time to express new growth. The forest floor, left to rot and reinvent itself is not dirt brown but the color of rich mulch covered everywhere with emerald and moss-colored ferns.

Beyond color is more to amaze: the trees create their own microclimate, pulling two thirds of their required water from the mists, fog and rain through the stomata of their awl-shaped leaves. This makes for an increase in humidity and a moist ground cover. And age: the California redwood is ancient among the ancients, an average life of five hundred years with some living into their third millennium. At the visitor center, a redwood that fell in 2006 was a sapling in 912AD. Markers along its rings show dates for the founding of Oxford University, Genghis Khan conquering Persia, the invention of the printing press and other world events. The tree was more than seven hundred years old when English Pilgrims first landed on the other end of the continent.

There are dozens of places to stop along the Avenue with informational signs, hiking trailheads or picnic tables. A driver could get through the Avenue in half an hour or spend all day giving in to the beckoning spots filled with green ferns, fallen trees now nesting new growth and a quiet unbothered by current events. According to one of the many roadside information signs, "[f]allen redwoods can take centuries to decompose. Generations of birds, small mammals, amphibians, and insects live and feed in cracks, crevices, and hollows. On the forest floor, redwood 'nurse logs' provide a fertile, moist growing surface for trees—including redwoods—and a variety of other plants such as huckleberry, ferns, and sorrel. In death, this is a redwood's legacy: new life."

Observing this life cycle gives a visitor even more to explore: banana slugs, squirrels, wild turkeys and other birds, and the occasional distant sight of a fox or black bear. High above, another biosphere exists with animals who's lives never make connection with the ground. So each glance upward at the high branches recalls lives outside our known world, the fleeting nature of our own selves and the continuity of the natural world despite our constant barrage of progress.

One of the major points along the Avenue is Founders' Grove where an easy half-mile walk informs visitors of the history of the park and the life cycle of the trees found there. In the center of the display is "Founders' Tree," reaching a height of three hundred and forty-six feet and one inch. The tree's circumference is forty feet and its first branch can be seen one hundred and ninety feet above. It isn't the tallest tree in the forest but it is an impressive one. It is here that the Latin name for the redwood makes sense: *sequoia sempervirens* or ever-living and where the threat to that appellation is most clear. Estimates are that in the early 1850's more than two million acres of old-growth redwoods existed in the fog belt of the northern coast. Less than sixty years later, it had been reduced by ninety-five percent.

It began first with the might of men and axe and saw in the middle of the nineteenth century. Old growth trees admired for the amount of board feet lumber they could produce were hacked down with relish. Walt Whitman made it sound illustrious when he wrote about "...the echo of teamsters' calls and the clinking chains, and the music of choppers' axes, the falling trunks and limbs, and the crash, the muffled shriek, the groan…" But he also portended the sad result "…as if voices ecstatic, ancient and rustling the century-lasting, unseen dryads, singing, withdrawing…"

Then the heroic age of felling by hand gave way to the "donkey engines" that cut through 600,000 board feet a day and indiscriminate deforesting left hillsides bare. Only in 1921, when a group of conservationists began to buy up swaths of acres, were the remaining woods preserved for visitors today. A visit to these redwoods is possible only because these visionaries sought the preservation of these trees. To tramp among them is to witness a wonder of the world, kept safe for our enjoyment and leisure.

If an explorer gets hungry, however, she should hope to have a picnic packed or a bit of luck because there are very few offerings of food for humans on this road. There is a bistro in Miranda and a seasonal hamburger stand in Phillipsville. Neither serves breakfast.

Toward the northern end of the route, in Redcrest, though, near an open air trinket mart selling Bigfoot key fobs and magnets made of redwood, and a shop with carvings from the gigantic burls, is The Eternal Tree Café. It is named for a nearby redwood, sporting a living but carved-out trunk that allows tourists to walk around inside. The restaurant is small and separate, enclosed in a glass sunroom, the kind that people in the midwest attach to their homes to stave off summer heat. The roof is glass and the walls are screened windows that are typically open in summer to let in a breeze. This and other businesses exist within the park and public land areas of Humboldt County, so must get licenses to operate and are limited to summer months to sell their goods.

Two women staff the café; they are not twins but they so reflect each other that they are difficult to recall as anything other than a couple of forest sprites. These are the dryads of whom Whitman spoke. Willowy and slim, each has her hair, once red but now a light gray tinged in tangerine, tied in a wispy, bun or careless braid. These small creatures are not young and beautiful, at least not in a modern way.

Instead, they are wrinkled and crepey, freckled from years outdoors, having lived in these forests for a long time. In place of green tunics, one sports a pair of overalls with a plaid shirt under, a bit disheveled and too loose for her frame. The other is in jeans worth a fortune in a second hand shop on Hollywood Boulevard: washed to a light blue over the years and a high-waisted reminder of the seventies when they were new.

They do not have the voices commonly assumed of young sprites because of course they are not young. These forest fairies are now aged and soon will be absorbed back into the forest from which they came. Each speaks with a rasp and a hardness to their voices that only smoke, whisky and time can produce. Joyous and raucous, they tease each other, the diners and the young bicyclists outside with just-ripped-from-the-calendars physiques. They laugh often and lean on each other for support in sisterly fashion.

They serve breakfast and lunch and a locally famous house-made blackberry cobbler topped with ice cream. One sprite, arriving late and driving a minivan, pulls up to fencing next door and, not slowing, plows into it, almost knocking it over. She has a twinkle in her eye and a little bloodshot to enhance it and she smiles broadly and puts her finger to her mouth as a sign of a conspiracy of silence with her about her little collision and perhaps a showing of her lack of sobriety. She and her sister cook and clean, serve and take orders, all while keeping a running narrative of good humor.

The food is good: fried eggs and bacon, toast and hashed brown potatoes. But the service is more memorable than the food and these two made the stop worth the price. The only thing they don't do is collect the money. For that, diners are forced next door into the gift shop to pay and peruse the souvenirs. The sprites' floor show is free.

The area along Highway 101, north of Fort Bragg and south of the rocky Oregon coastline is known as the California's "Lost Coast," a reputation partly from its remoteness and low population but also from the aura of its people—off the grid and often high. But it is a wondrous area, filled with legend, mystery and even a little magic. When it is time to leave this Shangri-La, and venture back to your journey north to

Oregon and the limits of California, back to reality, it is important to remember these woods, to hold them dear and assure their preservation. "The redwoods once seen, leave a mark or create a vision that stays with you always…from them comes silence and awe." Steinbeck warns us. But they also bring life, renewal and a couple of fairies from the forest.

*****

Connie Orozco-Morgan is on a journey to see the United States, writing about her experiences and the wonders of this country and its people. However, she misses her SWW colleagues and hope to stop by next time she is in town.

Second Place   **Terence Cady**

Transylvania
An Adventure in Old Europe

Romania's place in the Austro-Hungarian Empire ended in 1919, as did the Austro-Hungarian Empire itself with the Treaty of Versailles following WWI, but today the visitor becomes immersed in the color and sensibility of *fin de siècle* Europe as fiddle and accordion play haunting Gypsy tunes in the decorative 19th century dining hall of the Hotel Agape, in central Cluj-Napoca, a prosperous university city of 350,000 with one of the best medical schools in Europe.

In June 2014, my wife and I traveled to Transylvania, northern Romania, with a group of international folk dancers. Driving into the city from the airport, we joked about the "The People's Republic of Ugly" as we passed block after block of grim and decaying Soviet-style apartment buildings, still occupied.

In the old part of the city, the mostly old city, the landscape is dominated by 19th century buildings much like those in Prague or Paris, if you can visualize Paris in the middle of the 19th century, and not as the gleaming jewel it is today.

The City Center. Public squares, large and small, surrounded by cafes, hummed with relaxing students, couples, and families. One of the largest, St. Michael's Square, close to the Agape, is dominated by the monumental equestrian statue of Matthias Corvinus, born in Cluj and King of Hungary and Croatia from 1458-1490, and by the Gothic style Roman Catholic Church of St. Michael, begun in 1442. At night, folk ensembles in elaborate ethnic costumes, accompanied by folk musicians, entertain crowds with traditional Romanian songs. On weekends, the square is ringed with vendors selling everything from fresh flavorful produce to native crafts, and lots of "relics" featuring the image of Vlad the Impaler – Count Dracula.

A stroll through the city reveals an infrastructure little changed from WWII and left to further decay by forty years of Communism. Electrical wiring is strung outside buildings in crude bundles, and much of it appears to have been jerry-rigged. Many streets and sidewalks are in disrepair. Plaster on many buildings is peeling or has fallen out in chunks. Crude graffiti is ubiquitous. Yet, for a romantic sensibility, an old-world charm pervades the city which lies sheltered in a picturesque narrow valley bordered by farmlands instead of urban sprawl.

Lodging. All but the newest hotels are from an earlier era. Ours, The Agape, off St. Michael's Square, was excellent – four stars, by Romanian standards. Online reviews of the hotel are mixed. The most accurate one is a rebuttal to a disenchanted woman from Los Angeles, California, naturally. "Remember, you *are* in Eastern Europe." I would add, "not St. Tropez." The Agape is clean and the staff friendly and efficient. The elevator to all five floors was small and worked, albeit slowly. But who's going anywhere in a hurry? The rooms and the balconies, brightly adorned by potted flowers, surround an unroofed central courtyard which looks down on a glass atrium.

The walls and ceilings of the spacious main dining room are painted in a vivid style reminiscent of the embroidery found on ethnic costumes. As part of our tour perks, gifted musicians played hot Gypsy tunes nightly, a heady brew of Klezmer and the hot jazz of Django Reinhardt and Stefan Grappelli. Also "heady" were the copious amounts of homemade wines served with dinner *and* lunch, and shots of *Tuica*, a bright-hot clear liquid like Slivovitz, also homemade. The food was traditional, mostly Hungarian fare. Heavy on red meat, but fish and chicken were available, as well as *mamaliga*, made from semolina like Italian polenta, but tasting like cheese grits.

Dietary considerations. Vegetarians and the "gluten free" will have a difficult time. "So, what is 'vegetarian' and 'gluten free,' the waiters asked, but when told they readily accommodated by going to the kitchen and quickly returning with non-breaded zucchini and fish.

Legacy of the Holocaust. The atmosphere in the city and the hotel inspired grim jokes about feeling as though we were in Romania just before the war. "Which war?" someone quipped. It could as easily have been WWI as WWII. We were tempted to look around for clandestine operatives from the Austro-Hungarian Empire -- or the Third Reich.

The latter was not a joking matter. An informed traveler cannot escape the fact that Romania was one of the most virulent anti-Semitic arenas of the Holocaust. In a garden a block off St. Michael's Square is a memorial dedicated to the Jewish victims of the Holocaust from Cluj and the surrounding countryside. The memorial seems small and inconspicuous for a testament about such horrific events, but most shocking was the date on its base attesting to the fact that was erected there only one month before our visit.

A long-abandoned and decaying Synagogue sits nearby at the edge of the river Caffe. It was used as an assembly point for transported Jews who were not murdered outright by anti-Semitic thugs. A large wall with a locked gate surrounds the Synagogue. Next to the gate, an old couple sat in a dilapidated garden. Realizing the reason for our interest, they opened the gate allowing us to take a somber walk amid the shambles and weeds inside the wall. No Star of David or any sign that Jewish life existed here. And no memorial or sign indicating the infamy of the place.

The countryside of Transylvania is idyllic, a mixture of dense forests and agricultural fields, ringed by the Carpathian Mountains and the Transylvanian Alps, and dotted with farming towns and villages inhabited mostly by ethnic Hungarians and Saxons. (Before the dissolution of the Austro-Hungarian Empire, much of Transylvania was part of Hungary.) Traveling with an affinity group, in our case one comprised of dancers and musicians eager to learn local music and perform ethnic dances, provides an entrée into the cultural life of people whose lives are still governed by crops and seasons.

The people of Transylvania manifest a palpable pride and independence in their appearance and manners, which inoculated them against the Communist pressures that were brought to bear during the Soviet era. They are intensely proud of their cultural heritage, and each of the three villages we visited had a hall devoted to the local music, singing, dance and crafts.

Rupea. A partially restored fortress sits in splendor on a hill on the edge of the farming town of Rupea. The mayor and the local performance group greeted us wearing elaborately embroidered local costumes. Every village has its own style of traditional dress, though it requires special knowledge to distinguish the differences (or at least a visit to the ethnographic museum in Cluj). In any case, each style of dress is magnificent in its own way. The mayor of Rupea, a handsome man who had spent time in America and spoke excellent English, welcomed us with a speech about the Romanian Revolution of 1989, which ended collectivist agriculture and returned the land to the previous owners. As he spoke, handsome young men and beautiful young women circulated through the crowd offering freshly baked bread, plates of salt for dipping, and swigs of *Tuica* (clear for the men and cherry for the women) from a *plosca,* an elaborately painted, hand-carved communal flask.

Next, we waited in the center of town for "the cows to come home" -- literally. About a hundred milk cows, oxen, and cattle, came unled from a nearby pasture into the street, where they separated and went home, each going its own way by habit.

The first evening was spent in town. Dinner, dancing, drinking, and singing went late into the night with locals showing inexhaustible verve and visitors simply exhausted. The second night in Rupea was spent in a covered hall beside a lake. More feasting and dancing, with lots of boot slapping, drinking, toasting to American-Romanian friendship, and singing.

Lodging in Rupea was in a "hostel." We would call it a motel. It had a swimming pool and was spacious enough to accommodate a full-scale wedding. In the morning, we visited Rupea Fortress which has been partially restored, but not so much so that one could not appreciate the scars of past sieges and conquests. A local string quartet performed classical music for hours just inside the entrance. Families, including some with small children, gathered on the nearby grassy rise and listened with rapt attention.

Frata, in the Cluj region, is a small farming village. The main attraction is a diminutive ancient wooden church, common in Transylvania. The local priest explained the various religious themes of the nativist, almost primitive, hand-painted murals covering the walls and ceiling, and then informed us that the Roman and Orthodox Churches recently "merged" into a holy alliance more accommodating to the historical dualism of Roman and Orthodox Catholicism in Romania. Stepping outside, we could see grass being harvested with scythes. The villagers were delighted to have us try our hand at mowing. On the long walk back to the village center, we pass small farmhouses with chickens and pigs and flower gardens and receive friendly greetings at every turn.

Evening and another banquet, music and dancing in our honor. And more *tuica* and homemade wine. Several Gypsy families live in Frata. This is not typical in Romania where the Gypsy population remains an underclass and generally lives apart. Here, they seemed to be at ease, enjoying the banquet and performing for us along with the other dancers, much to everyone's delight. The music was by the *Soporul de Campie Band*, featuring the famous Romanian violinist Ciurcui Alexandru, aka *Sandorica*.

Marisel. The road from the Transylvanian plains to Marisel winds up through mountain meadows in the *Apsueni* mountains reminiscent of the landscape in "The Sound of Music." Wooden houses sprinkle the slopes. Although it is summer, it is cool here and smoke from wood fires rises from chimneys. Transport from the village center to the festival hall is by horse drawn carts with rubber wheels. As we gather in a meadow adjacent to the dining hall, set on another slope, women in ethnic costume blow on huge alpine horns. What are these horns used for? Our tour guide, a native Romanian, joked: They are sending a message: "Come now. My husband is not home."

While our dinner cooked in a huge cast iron pot on a tripod over an open fire, we perused a selection of local craft items, drank the *tuica* that our hosts pressed on us, and snacked on tempting local cheeses. If you are on a diet, Romania might not be right for you. Our superb dinner was followed by lively dancing with the villagers around a huge bonfire in the meadow.

Other attractions: *Sambata de Jos* **Stud Farm.** Horses are bred and trained here for the famous Spanish Riding School in Vienna. Magnificent beasts, well-advanced in their training, perform to the music of Johann Strauss on an open parade ground. After the performance, we toured the numerous barns which house in separate stalls the best breeding horses and we visited the corral where the babies came up to the fence, hoping to be petted.

Brancoveanu **Monastery.** The nearby *Brancoveanu* Monastery is a marvelous white Medieval complex, rebuilt in the 17th century. Approaching the monastery on a long tree-lined path, one faces a stunning view of alpine mountains and meadows. Inside the gates, hand-painted murals and frescoes, mostly in blue hues, adorn the exterior walls and interiors of the many buildings. Words cannot convey the beauty and power of the religious themes of the work. Nor can photographs capture the scale and scope of the place. The monastery deserves a full day.

Bran Castle. "Dracula's Castle," the model for Bram Stoker's famous story, lies in the region of Brasov in the Transylvanian Alps. This magnificent fortress, set high on a steep rocky hill, was the home of the beloved Queen Marie of Romania, who reigned in the early 20th century. The real Count Dracula (Vlad Țepeș, Vlad III, Prince of Wallachia, 1431–1476/77), posthumously dubbed Vlad the Impaler, never lived in the castle, and never conquered it. The hike from the base to the castle is steep and requires strong legs, but efforts have been made to accommodate the disabled.

Salina Turda Salt Mine. Who wants to visit a salt mine? We were dubious, but it was spectacular! Mining here began around 1200 A.D. and operated until recently. The scale is comparable to Carlsbad

Caverns in New Mexico, but the lowest chamber, accessible by treacherous, slippery footpaths or by a tiny elevator, rivals the largest in Carlsbad Caverns. The massive chamber is lit by a dazzling display of fluorescent lights arranged to create an unearthly aura, and it houses a playground, complete with miniature golf, boat rides, and a Ferris wheel. While amusing for visitors, the area was designed for asthmatic children who are treated therapeutically in the clean, salty atmosphere of the mine. As a special treat, our tour guides arranged for a concert by a string quartet which played Brahms' quartets in the underground amphitheater.

Ethnograpic museums. These vary in size and content, from displays of art, pottery, textiles, and ethnic costumes to crafts and farm tools, and every city and sizeable town seems to have one, often doubling as performance and social centers. The museums often feature rare, striking collections of photographs of early village life.

On the outskirts of Cluj, the Romulus Vuia National Ethnographic Park sits amid acres of undisturbed meadowland, and features original and authentically reconstructed buildings – homes, barns, and an ancient chapel, transporting you to a time when life was solely agrarian.

The population in the cities is a mixed bag. Many embrace the new freedoms, especially the freedom to travel abroad. Many of the talented performance groups we met can now travel outside Romania and welcome the change. Others, those less able to adapt to the new, mostly market economy, miss the "old days," when they were guaranteed work, even menial work, and were afforded the "luxury" of two weeks vacation at a Soviet resort on the Black Sea. These are the older, shabbily dressed people with the worn grocery bags and sad faces.

Money and Language. Romanian is a Romance, Latin-based language, a hybrid of Italian and an indigenous Daco language. It's tricky, but a few basic words and phrases can be learned with little effort, and its use by tourists is much appreciated. The educated and most people in commerce speak English and German. Some of the older folks probably speak Russian as well.

Although Romania is a member of the European Union where the Euro predominates, Romania adheres to the Romanian *Lei*. The exchange rate was about three *Lei* to the US dollar, a good travel value. Credit cards are accepted, and ATMs are common.

The cities are wired for Wi-Fi, virtually everywhere, more so than in the US. Not so in the countryside, but there is access in the larger towns.

Telephone service by cell phone is easy, even in the countryside, provided you left home with an application or service enhancement that permits international calls.

Romania today, 2022. Romania is still emerging from the horrors of WWII and from forty years of communism under Soviet puppet dictators. In 1989, the last of these, Nicolae Ceaușescu and his wife, were summarily executed against a wall in Bucharest. Thus began the transformation of Romania, now a part of the European Union, into a fledgling democracy, a transformation that is a work in progress and far from being realized.

And today, Romania, a member of the European Union and a member of NATO, is a host to refugees from Russia's war on Ukraine. Today is probably not a good time to visit Romania unless one wants to experience the chaos caused by war, or perhaps to help the refugees.

*****

Background reading: Balkan Ghosts, A Journey Through History, by Richard D. Kaplan, Picador, St. Martin's Press, 1993.

*****

Interesting links.

http://www.romaniatourism.com/
http://www.romaniatourism.com/practical-information.html
http://www.tripadvisor.ca/Tourism-g294457-Romania-Vacations.html
http://wikitravel.org/en/Romania
http://www.hoteltravel.com/romania/guides/travel_tips.htm
http://www.virtualtourist.com/travel/Europe/Romania/Municipiul_Bucuresti/Buchar est-520545/Warnings_or_Dangers-Bucharest-TG-C-1.html

*****

Terence Gilmore Cady is a recovering trial lawyer and a nationally certified specialist in child welfare law. He has written two novels, one published, four published short stories, four published poems, one of which was a finalist among six nominated in 2019 for the Pushcart Prize in poetry *Fear of Fire, Lower East Side, 1966.*

Third Place   **Vicky Ramakka**

Night Photography in
Joshua Tree National Park

Laid back mornings, intense evenings is the best way the describe the night photography workshop my husband and I attended at Joshua Tree National Park. Four days to explore, admire, learn about and photograph the remarkable vegetation in this transition zone where the Mojave Desert meets the Colorado Desert. What a treat.

We drove 700 miles from northwest New Mexico to participate in the Bradley Photographic Light and Shape workshop. Traveling through the Mojave desert on the way to Twentynine Palms tends to turn pre-conceived images of California upside down. No surfers on the ocean, no lush fruit orchards. Instead, expansive views of desert habitat, interrupted by occasional detours to photograph the ephemeral blossoms of this arid landscape. It was our good fortune to be there during a peak year for California wildflowers.

The other 10 participants came from Canada, the East coast and California, where Jason Bradley is based. Our gathering point was the 29 Palms Inn with individual bungalows painted in desert colors and within walking distance of the Park's visitor center.

Workshop routine was to meet at Jason's, the workshop leader, bungalow mid-morning to review and edit mages under the guidance of his two assistant instructors. More formal presentations occurred before and after lunch on photographic techniques as well as software processing to bring out the best in images. Mid-afternoon brought a scurry to gather gear and drive into the park. We practiced daylight shooting of wildflowers along one of the developed trials, then moved to another location for a boxed dinner and night photography.

Joshua Tree may be one of the greatest misnomers of the plant world. Not trees at all, *Yucca brevifolia* is in the Agave family. Granted, they are very *big* succulents, generally growing 20 to 40 feet tall. The name comes from 1800s Mormon explorers who likened the outstretched branches to the biblical figure Joshua, leading them along their journey. Native American residents used the flower buds and seeds as a food source. The massive, football-size flower clusters are pollinated during night visits by the yucca moth.

In 2019, Joshua Tree was the 11th most visited national park, with nearly 3 million visitors. While more than half of the park is designated wilderness, we found the sections of the park where we photographed easy to access with paved roads, trails well-signed, and tolerably decent restrooms at most parking areas. The Cholla Cactus Garden trail is a good place to see many of the park's fifteen cactus species. Wise visitors take heed of warning signs about the Teddybear or Jumping Cholla, *Cylindropuntia bigelovii. During one workshop session, we had a lengthy discussion on ways to survive a teddybear attack.*

Our first evening excursion was to practice silhouettes and light painting. Even though Joshua Tree is designated as a dark sky park, there was noticeable light pollution from Palm Springs and towns beyond the park's boundaries. Framing a Joshua Tree against the sky and greatly underexposing this subject produced unique silhouettes with soft golden back light.

Numerous websites, as well as YouTube videos, provide instructions on night photography and guidance on camera gear. Good sources to start with are: www.outdoorphotographer.com/tips-techniques/nature-landscapes/night-landscape-photography and www.diyphotography.net/properly-shoot-landscape-night-photography .

For light painting, Jason used an LED flashlight to evenly light an especially symmetrical specimen from bottom to top, right side to left. An uneven, jerky painting effort would produce a lopsided image, with some branches disappearing into the dark. While actual shooting time was in seconds, it took many attempts to obtain a satisfactory result. Furthermore, coordination is required such that everyone opens shutters at the same time; then headlamps or small flashlights are used in between exposures for making camera adjustments. Thus, it would be nearly midnight before we dragged back to our lodging. But not to bed yet, batteries needed to be charged, images downloaded for morning reviews, gear cleaned and made ready for the next day.

The Cap Rock Trail, named for the rock formation resembling (what else), a brimmed hat, was an easy, well-groomed, nearly level path allowing quiet meandering among the park's namesake. This was the site of an evening's shoot in which Kevin Osborn, one of the workshop instructors, performed a bit of technological wizardry to recreate a Giant Sloth that may have roamed the park a few thousand years ago.

He demonstrated a Pixelstick, a 6-foot long bar, slim enough to wrap a hand around, with LED lights along it length. The lights are pre-programed and manipulated via a small controller attached to the stick to flash in certain sequences and colors. While our eyes saw intermittent light bursts in front of Kevin's dark form walking slowly behind trees, our camera sensors recorded the magical shape of the prehistoric creature.

Photography workshops can be intense. Be prepared to fully engage in exhausting but worthwhile pursuit of treasured images from exotic places you have never visited before. Enjoy the camaraderie of other participants who likely have similar interests and love of the outdoors. Layer on clothes—it gets cold when the sun goes down and standing for an hour or two behind a tripod does not generate body warmth. Wear good hiking shoes, to handle uneven ground and not worry too much if something slithers by. A Hoodman Loop is handy for daytime shooting, a small magnifier in a tube that fits over the back screen of a camera to review images, which otherwise are hard to see in bright sunlight.

All too often Joshua Trees are called bizarre, odd, weird. But stepping away from the other participants, it's easy to feel a certain amount of companionship with these Joshua Trees with their upright "arms." Looking over our images from the workshop triggers pleasant memories of this enchanting environment.

*****

Vicky Ramakka's first novel *The Cactus Plot* won the NM-AZ Book Award for cozy mystery and reached best seller on Amazon. A sequel, *The Pearl Plot*, will be released in early 2023. Through photography and writing, Vicky shares her love of the southwest in magazine articles and on her website, https://vrwriting.net.

Night Photography in Joshua National Park, was first published in *Cactus and Succulent Journal*, Spring 2021. This article is slightly revised from the original.

Section Thirteen

Non-Fiction– Memoir

Always the most popular category in the annual writing contest, our reviewers have a tough time combing through these tales of personal experiences.   We had a lot of excellent writing to choose from among the entries.

Memoirs are stories based on personal experiences. What we look for is emotional drive – why does this memory stay with the author enough to make them need to recount it – why should their audience care?   How the story is told is more interesting than the bare facts.

First Place   **Ruth Marshall**

Forever

Bartering Lesson

The loquat tree in our backyard grew bigger than the other fruit trees. I believe it had his feet below our compost pile, maybe the neighbor's one too because, according to my father, it grew over 30 feet tall.

In early summers, my mother would shoo us out the door after lunch to go eat our dessert up the loquat tree. Three of my four brothers, Arturo, Harry and Benjamin in their overalls and I, not hampered in the least by my dress, would swing up the branches like twittering monkeys. Our little brother, Carlitos, wanted to go, but had to take a nap. My mother would put him in his bed and sing to him, as she had done with her lovely soothing voice for each of us in turn. Clearly, he was her favorite, with his golden, curly hair and eyes even bluer than my father's. We didn't mind, we liked him too. People in the small town where we grew up had made him their human mascot and stopped to pet him every time my mother took him along when shopping. "An angel," they would say. "Too beautiful for this world."

Glad that we were old enough not to have to take naps, each of us would find a space on a branch, no specific boundaries, whoever got to it first owned it for the time it took to stuff ourselves with the yellow fruit --the tender, juicy flesh contrasting with the rounded, pebble-like seeds, shiny and smooth that we rolled in our mouths just for the feeling before spitting them out to the ground, or using them as projectiles to the closest sibling. We talked kid's stuff, we laughed at our jokes, and we ate and we spit. We were the Four Musketeers. And we were forever.

The neighbors next door were not very friendly. I think they were better off than my parents. Their kids would look at the loquat tree through the spaces between the slats of the wood fence separating the properties, with wistful looks and frequent lip wiping on the back of their hands. We never thought of bringing fruit down to share with them.

Until the day one of the kids offered something in exchange for loquats.

I was quick to climb down to check the item being held for inspection between the fence boards --a magazine with a black and white picture of Elizabeth Taylor, all shiny eyes and hair and half smiling at me. I gave him the few loquats I had in the small pocket of my dress, promised him more, and grabbed the magazine with sticky hands. I smiled back at the picture, unaware of the contrast between my snaggletooth smile and stringy hair and the glossy promise of what I could become.

The next day, another item. My brothers caught on and began stuffing their pockets before coming down. Since my dress did not have big pockets, I found a small basket with an arched handle that I held with my teeth going up and down the tree.

What a business! The loot: books, toys, porcelain figurines of kids and animals, rings and necklaces that needed a lot of going up the tree for more basketfuls of fruit. The four of us liked best the glass marbles that held within swirly worlds of colors and shapes and competed fiercely each time one was offered as barter.

And one day, no more. Instead, their grandmother came to the fence yelling, with her mouth opened so wide she scared the hell out of us. On the rare occasions when she had bothered to speak in our direction, she had been soft spoken, yet had managed to impart terror and utter respect.

She wanted everything back. We refused, trembling all the way to our bare feet, and told her that we had gotten everything in fair exchange.

She visited our parents demanding retribution. Our parents, unaware of our dealings, asked us what it was all about. After our fervent explanations, they all followed us to the storage shed that was set way back in the property, past the orchard. When we did something wrong, like playing or fighting on our father's newly prepared vegetable beds, the punishment was to lock the guilty one, sometimes all of us, in the old shed for a couple of hours to let us think about and repent our transgressions. It was a scary place, dark when the door was closed, with only faint light coming from a small window placed high on the wall, the panes grimy and crisscrossed with spider webs. I didn't mind it too much. The place was full of stuff, including an ancient Remington typewriter. I used to pound down the letter keys to make their rusted levers lift and strike the roller, and then pretend I was writing poems or something about the images floating around in my head.

When everyone had squeezed in, we started, as slowly as we could get away with, to uncover the treasures stored in boxes, each clearly marked with our name.

They made us return everything, which we did tearful at the injustice of it all. But I still had the first magazine --the one with Elizabeth Taylor on the cover-- hidden under my bed.

That was the end of the bartering business. We never shared a loquat with the neighbor's kids again, though I always felt they were ready to barter all over again. Not us. No way.

But all that happened the year before the fateful spring day when everything changed.

*****

Fateful Day

I stayed home from school that day with the pretense of an upset stomach. I knew the teacher was having a review of a History lesson that had been particularly boring, but I wasn't about to tell my mother that. After a couple of hours, tired of staying in bed, I got up and told Mother that I was feeling better and asked if she needed help. She gave me the 'you-did-it-again' look and told me to get Carlitos from the play yard and tell my father that lunch was almost ready. My brother liked to hide, so I called him as I got closer to the shaded fenced area to give him time to run behind the chestnut tree. He wasn't there.

I kept calling and looking under and behind everything big enough to hide him. I went in the garage where Father was soldering the broken plow Mr. Loyola had brought in for repair, and that he needed urgently, I heard him say, to get the ground ready for planting the summer crops. I told Father about lunch being ready and asked if Carlitos was in the garage with him, maybe hiding, because he wasn't in his play yard.

"No, I haven't seen him. Not since breakfast." He frowned and quickly turned the torch and a couple of valves off. We checked every corner of the garage, then we stood looking over the downward slope of the rest of the property. The wood shed, filled with stacks of split wood for the cooking stove was surrounded on three sides by the vegetable garden where plants were already growing in neat rows. A path divided the yard all the way down to the orchard, now in bloom, that offered fragrant, private spaces where I hid whenever I had a new book or magazine, so my mother could not ask me to stop reading and help her with the chores. I went inside the shed to look behind the wood stacks, came out shaking my head at my father who was standing by the tall gate of the fenced area where a concrete cistern served as a storage tank to water the vegetable garden and as a pool for us big kids to splash about and cool off in the summer. I went to look behind the big artichoke plants lining one side of the garden, then I kept walking toward the orchard. He had to be there.

I turned around as if on wheels when I heard the terrible wail.

My father was holding Carlitos in his arms, and my little brother looked awful, his head bent far back, eyes closed, golden hair and soggy clothes streaming water down my father's arms. And my father's eyes were wild.

He ran to the house, silent now, with me at his heels, water drops off my brother's hair and clothes falling hard on my face. He found my mother in one of the bedrooms and, without saying a word, placed Carlitos in her arms, turned and run out the door. The familiar sound of the old Plymouth starting came through the open window, while I stared at my mother now sitting on the bed trying to take the wet clothes off my brother, as if he had been caught in the rain and needed warmth.

My father came back without the doctor but with Mr. Leiba. I think he was a medical person who assisted the only doctor in town and sometimes helped our local veterinary. He turned Carlitos on his stomach, pressing hard on his back, then gently turned him over and lifted one of his eyelids, I saw a flash of blue and started to say something, but Mr. Leiba shook his head. He was just going through the motions, for he knew death when he saw it.

Later, my mother, hands trembling, wrote a note and a list of names of relatives and friends who lived in other towns and sent me to the telegraph office. Weaving my way through the kids going home from school for their lunch break, I saw Benjamin walking with his friends. As usual, he was joking and laughing, but the laughter froze when he saw my face.

"What's the matter?"

I motioned him away from his friends and told him. Giving me a look of disbelief, he was running home before I could finish the telling.

I opened the post office door and headed for the telegraph window. Miss Idilia Loyola, wife of Mr. Loyola--the one with the broken plow-- gave me her usual welcoming smile. I handed her the piece of paper, watching the smile vanish as she read the fateful words. She looked older somehow when she started tapping the keys, the staccato sound sealing the still-unbelieved message in my brain.

By nightfall the whole town knew. My aunt Luisa had come and taken over, as was her way, her big eyes wet like dark pools. My barely contained tears overflowed when I saw Carlitos lying on a table that had been set up in the living room. He was covered half-way up with a white sheet, hands folded over the small chest, and his face exposed and asleep. Because my uncle run the power plant, I guess, my aunt had him string bare electric bulbs from the ceiling, hanging low over my brother, giving his face an eerie cast. Candles would have been nicer, I thought, but my aunt must know better. I stood leaning on a wall, eyes tightly closed, wishing with all my being for my brother to wake up.

"Not long for this world," I had heard people say earlier, shaking their heads while peering through the opened doors and windows, taking in our way of life and repeating like a litany "Too beautiful a child. An angel he looked like," while leaving small bunches of flowers on door steps and window sills.

I do not remember the rest of that night, just waking up the next morning, hungry and cold, lying on the floor in a corner of the living room, with a cushion under my head and covered with a blanket somebody had placed on me. And with the memories of an awful dream that the pervading smell of iris and lilacs placed in vases around my brother soon turned real.

The day started calm and clear, turning windy and bringing clouds in the afternoon when almost everyone in town followed the open cart pulled by one horse and carrying my brother in his white coffin. Walking alongside the cart with my brothers, I caught whiffs of the fresh paint when gusts of wind slid over the small box.

I saw my father walking alone behind the cart, everyone giving him space upon seeing the grief on his face. My mother, almost hidden from view by the women surrounding her and supported by my aunt, followed. I could hear her crying softly in those moments when the wind stilled between gusts.

Ahead, past the town outskirts, the cemetery gates stood open. I slowed my steps, moving slightly aside to let the procession pass. My brothers looked back questioning, but I motioned with my hand for them to keep going. I saw the cart go in and waited until the last person disappeared behind the oak trees that lined the gravel road to the graves before sitting down on the slatted wood bench outside the gates. I raised my face to the stormy sky, closed my eyes and prayed.

I gave it all. With the incurable faith of the young, I prayed certain that my brother would come back to me, whole, blue eyes open, looking at me with a new brilliance from their glimpse of heaven. The Fifth Musketeer. What a surprise it will be for everyone coming out of the cemetery! The smile restored on my father's face. Songs back on my mother's lips.

I felt my father's arms lifting me from the bench. He carried me home in a tight embrace, my head resting on his shoulder, eyes now wide open looking at the people following in a reverse procession that kept shedding them off as they neared their homes.

My brothers walked at our father's side, close enough to touch him, Benjamin, now the youngest, holding on to the jacket. The *being forever* feeling lost, vanished with the wind.

*****

Ruth H. Marshall says her writing was born from a love of reading in her native language, Spanish. Before coming to America, she wrote over 50 radio scripts of stories geared to children in rural schools in Chile. Now, after many years of reading in English and learning the craft, she has started writing again.

Second Place   **Paula Nixon**

Ursa Major

The black bear is a species, Ursus americanus, not a color.
Linda Masterson, *Living With Bears Handbook*

The pile of scat was dry and crumbly, not thirty feet from the back of my house. I used a stick to break it apart and found it was full of small brown shells. Later, from an upstairs bathroom window, I looked down on a spot where the bear might have paused to eat nuts—a clearing in a semicircle of piñon trees, the bare ground scattered with empty pine cones.

On long winter nights, at that same window, I gaze up at shining Orion and wonder where the bear is sleeping. Does he ever dream about his earliest days?

January 1995
Somewhere in the forest, high on the mountain above Santa Fe, two tiny newborn black bear cubs—a male and a female, each about the size of a chipmunk—snuggled next to their mother nursing while she slept soundly in a warm, dry den that she had dug in the fall.

*****

Daylight was fading when Dave and I stepped out of the SUV at the side of a dirt road about two miles north of the Santa Fe Plaza. We followed the realtor—long blond hair, jeans tucked into fancy cowboy boots—a few feet down the slope. She stopped and made a sweeping gesture with her right arm—*this* is the place to build a new house with a view to the west of the Jemez Mountains. At the other end of the lot tucked in among the juniper and piñon trees was a 50-year-old New Mexican-style bungalow. On our quick walk-through we noted sagging beams, stained carpet, ancient appliances and the faint smell of wood smoke and wet dog. Every inch of it needed renovation.

That night over dinner we debated our choices—a single-family home on a tidy street, a new townhouse behind a popular pottery market, or the rundown house in the woods. After dinner we set out to drive by the last property for another look, but couldn't find the dirt road in the dark. Back at the bed and breakfast we shivered and paused to gaze up at the full moon high overhead with a ring around it. We made an offer on the fixer-upper on the big lot with a view the next morning before catching our return flight to Texas.

*****

Back to Houston, back to work. We didn't have the means or a plan yet to make a move to New Mexico. In March we visited for the first time since closing on the house. After landing in Albuquerque, we stopped for enchiladas and a margarita and then drove the 65 miles to Santa Fe. This time we found the dirt road without a problem and pulled into the driveway marked by a tall cottonwood that was near dead, although it would be months before we realized it. The squat, flat-roofed house didn't have an ounce of charm. The dumpalow, Dave called it. We pulled in under the carport and Dave jumped out to unload—suitcases, cots, and sleeping bags—ready to set up for the weekend. I reclined my seat and refused to get out of the car.

*****

By late May the mother bear and her two cubs left their den. It was a tough time of year for the female who needed to protect her nursing cubs and look for food to replenish her depleted fat stores. After she found a sturdy tree and taught the cubs, each weighing about five pounds, to climb, she had a safe place for them to stay while she ventured off—not too far—to forage for grass and dandelions, to turn over rocks and logs on the hunt for ants and insects.

*****

On our second visit, over Memorial Day weekend, my folks drove down from Denver to meet us. We had a new bed, our first piece of furniture, delivered shortly before they arrived. Dad brought his surveying equipment and we spent a chilly day in rain and sleet shooting elevations—Dad at the tripod, Dave toting the rod in the trees—getting a feel for the shape and contour of the long narrow lot that was now ours. Mom and I braved the kitchen with its chipped asbestos floor tile and plywood countertops to make pimento cheese sandwiches out of a jar.

After dinner in town, Dave lit a fire in the living room kiva and we pulled lawn chairs close, the house more endearing in firelight.

*****

The subdivision, Colonia Solana, was created in the late 1940s in the foothills of the Sangre de Cristo Mountains. Back then the dirt road ended at our driveway. Four modest pumice block houses, covered with stucco in varying shades of brown had been built on one- to two-acre lots on the west side of the road. Prior owners had planted fruit trees and rose bushes, irises and lilacs. By the time we purchased the house, the road was cut through and climbed higher into the foothills where new homes were springing up every month.

In the fall of 1997 we made the move, thrilled to escape the endless humid summers, snarled traffic, and dull routine of corporate jobs. The little house overflowed with our furniture and unpacked moving boxes. We set up a makeshift office in the sunroom. Most of Dave's architectural consulting work would be out of state; Santa Fe would be our home base. No time to focus on a remodeling project, we improvised. Our three senior cats—Misha, Paris, Moet—each claimed a favorite spot. One perched on top of a stack of boxes, another snoozed on a sunny corner of a desk, the third napped in a tangle of blankets on the unmade bed.

I relied on a field guide to learn the names of birds that stopped by the platform feeders—weathered and warped scraps of plywood nailed on top of fence posts—outside our kitchen window: scrub jays, two kinds of towhees, chickadees, and flickers. Coyotes yipped and howled at night, but we rarely saw them. I never suspected it, but a bear likely considered our yard part of its extended territory during the summer, passing through on the lookout for an easy meal.

*****

The two bear cubs born in the winter of 1995 were now on their own. They had hibernated with their mother for a second winter, but she shooed them off early the next summer when she went looking for a mate. The female cub was allowed to stay close to her mother's territory, but the male was expected to move on. After their first summer alone—fattened up on acorns, chokecherries, and wild berries—they both dug dens and settled in for the winter.

*****

We knew it was past time to start the renovation once we had to climb a ladder to shovel the flat roof every time it snowed. Dave drew up plans and hired a contractor who immediately demolished most of the roof structure. At the beginning of July, right on schedule, the monsoon season started. The crew of two guys would no sooner remove the blue tarp and set to work framing the parapet walls when black clouds would move in and the scent of rain would fill the air, often forcing them to unroll the tarp and call it a day.

Dave and I holed up in the second bedroom, as far from the construction as we could get, with our two remaining cats. We covered our bed each morning with a sheet of plastic. By the time the new millennium arrived, the dumpalow, now almost unrecognizable with its high ceilings and brand new kitchen, had been transformed into a cozy guest house. Warm and dry, we lifted a glass to welcome the New Year.

Early in the spring, after the winter weather had cleared, the contractor began the foundation for a new house. Nestled into the hill, it would have big windows facing west near the piece of ground where the realtor had stood five years earlier. For the better part of two years there was a crew on our lot. An ongoing commotion: the rumble of a concrete truck, the staccato thump of a nail gun, loud rock-n-roll from a beat-up radio.

And then it went quiet. We moved into the new house with our cat Misha, just turned twenty. Birds sang outside our kitchen window, perched in a tall piñon tree. We saw mule deer, coyotes, and the occasional bobcat pass through the yard. It turned out the wildlife used the same natural pathway—visible from our breakfast nook—that we had widened and now used as a driveway. But never a bear. When a neighbor told me his bird feeder had been destroyed, I dismissed the idea that it was a bear although I had heard reports: a bear napping by the river not far from the Plaza spotted by tourists from a bridge, a mother with her cubs cruising through town prompting a school lock down. They ventured into residential neighborhoods for the crabapples and cherries rotting on the ground under fruit trees, a bag of dog kibble stored on the patio, a leftover slice of pizza tossed in the trash.

It was late in the summer and had been raining. A recent story on the radio reported a bear wandering along the river, about a mile downhill from us grazing the fruit trees. But still I was shocked to look out the back door one evening to find that the bird feeders had been mangled, the suet gone, cages in the mud, hinges bent beyond repair.

I called New Mexico Game and Fish to report the bear visit, not really sure what I expected them to do. The wildlife officer who returned my call was firm. No bird feeders in the summer. No trash outside before the morning of pickup day.

The bear came back every year. I learned to look and listen for the signs. Scat, of course. But also missing apples from one day to the next on the ground under a gnarled tree that rarely fruited. A midmorning commotion at a neighbor's collection of metal trashcans.

*****

A few years later Dave was sketching the next phase of home improvements. Fences and walls. I agreed we needed them, but didn't want to inhibit animals from passing through the yard. His solution was a three-foot wide opening in the far corner of the back fence. Not visible from the house it gave our secretive wild neighbors access through a wooded area. A quick scoot across the gravel driveway and they could head on up the mountain. The new opening was the perfect place to set my remote camera. Wary of surprising a bear I always made noise when I ventured into the trees, usually a rock in each hand banged together to mimic the ursine habit of popping its jaws to let others know where it is. After I set the automatic shutter, it didn't take long for the camera feed to be filled with pictures of skunks, raccoons, and rabbits.

Finally, on a September day, eighteen years after I stepped out of the realtor's SUV, I saw the bear. Not in person, but in a shot captured on my camera. Down on all fours, a fine-looking furry bear—more brown than black, rounded ears, pointy snout—walking through the opening in the fence. He had passed through in the morning, about the time I eat breakfast, but never made a sound.

*****

Paula Nixon holds a business degree from the University of Kansas. She has published work with *Earth Island Journal, Sun Magazine, Santa Fe Reporter, Albuquerque Journal, SouthWest Sage,* among others. She lives and works in Santa Fe, New Mexico

Third Place   **Evelyn Neil**

Bubble Gum

Sweet treats are rare during the sugar rationing years of World War II. So news of the arrival of bubble gum at the Piggly Wiggly store travels fast in my Wyoming prairie town. Each customer is allowed just one piece while the supply lasts.

"Take Jay with you. Get a piece for him." Our mother hands me two pennies. "Hurry before Mr. Dorf sells out."

"Why do I always have to take him?"

"Because I told you to. That's why."

Mother buttons Jay into his brown winter coat. He fusses and squirms as she ties the strings of the sheepskin ear flaps on his cap under his chin. The rabbit-fur-trimmed hood on my red wool coat tickles my ears as I pull it onto my head. I grab my almost four-year-old brother's grubby hand and yank him out the front door.

"Come on. We have to hurry."

"Be nice, Eva. Remember your manners," says Mother.

The March wind cuts through my coat and rabbit fur mittens. Corn snow pelts my face as I pull Jay along the two blocks to the grocery store. There are already lots of kids in line at the counter when we enter the warm store with its jumbled smells of damp wool, oiled hardwood floors and cigarette smoke.

Waiting our turn, I stand on one foot and then the other. What's taking so long? Bored, I twist around and check out the store. The baskets of potatoes and onions look different from the ones stored in wood boxes in the dirt cellar under our house. No white spouts are growing out of these. Wood shelves lining the walls sag under the weight of cans of fruits and vegetables, each with a brightly printed picture label to show what's inside. Mother cans the fruits and vegetables from her garden in see-through glass jars with screw-on lids.

In the stack of fifty-pound bags of flour I spot a pink and blue print fabric like the one Mother used to make me a summer play dress.

At the back of the store Mr. Joiner, the butcher stands at the heavy wood block chopping up dead chickens with a shiny cleaver. I wonder if they ran around with blood spurting out their headless necks like the chickens do in our back yard when Mother cuts their heads off. Maybe he grabs them by the head and flips them around to twist their necks like my grandma does. He looks up and winks and waves. I wave back.

On days when I shop for Mother, I never go into the back of the store but wait at the counter for Mr. Dorf to gather the things on her list. Next year when I'm in first grade, I'll learn to read the grocery list and be able to pick the items off the shelves myself. I won't have to wait for Mr. Dorf to finish with the other customers. Some days Mother orders so many things, I have to make two or three trips to carry it all home. Maybe I'll ask Santa for a wagon.

"Eva." Jay tugs my coat sleeve.

"One piece for you, little man and one piece for you, young lady." I hand Mr. Dorf the two pennies. "Oh, Eva, take this box of salt. I forgot to put it in your mother's order yesterday." he says. "Next? Only five pieces left."

I wrap my arm around the blue salt container with the picture of the little girl holding her umbrella in the rain and hold out my free hand to my little brother.

"Give me your bubble gum so you don't drop it on the way home." I clench my fingers around the waxy-paper wrapped treasures. "Follow me. I can't hold your hand."

Our cousin, Jim, who is six like me, comes into the store as the last piece of Double Bubble is handed over the counter. Tears trickle down his ruddy cheeks. His nose begins to run.

"Come on. We'll share," I say. He stops crying and wipes his nose on the sleeve of his navy pea coat. We push out of the steamy, crowded store and run up Main Street toward the Ranger Hotel.

"Let's go in here," I say.

The three of us push and push until finally the heavy revolving glass door to the lobby of the four-story building turns. Once inside, Jim runs to an over-stuffed couch in the corner by the sputtering steam radiator.

"No one will see us here," he says.

We climb onto the soft brown sofa to enjoy our strawberry-flavored treats. I remove the wrapper from the first piece and hand it to Jay who shoves the sugary morsel into his mouth and begins to chew. Juice from the huge pink wad runs out the corners of his mouth and drips down the front of his coat and onto the sofa.

I unwrap the other piece of Double Bubble and put it to my nose. I should give half to Jim. After all, I said we'd share. But its sugary strawberry scent is too much to resist. I pop the whole piece into my mouth and chew. I carefully smooth both wrappers and look at the comics printed on the inside. I'll take them home and beg our older sister, Marj to read them to us at bedtime. Jim sniffles and squirms until it's his turn. With sticky fingers and juice dripping off our chins, we chatter, giggle and share the treats until Mr. Chamberlain, the hotel owner, comes to where we're sitting.

"All right, kids, time to go home."

I don't understand why he is so gruff, but slide off the couch and tuck the container of salt under my arm. "Come, guys, let's go." I reach for Jay's sticky hand. Jim, who is the first out the door, runs up the street toward his home.

When Jay and I enter our kitchen where Mother is peeling potatoes, she asks, "Did you get your bubble gum?" What a silly question. She can see we are still chewing and Jay has sticky pink drool on his chin.

*****

Two nights later, as the wind howls and slams the falling snow against the window panes, I awake and cry out, "My throat hurts."

Mother, engulfed in her ever-present scent of cigarettes, whiskey and *Evening in Paris,* appears at my bedside in her long silky blue nightgown. She places her cool soft hand on my forehead.

"You're burning up." She goes into the bathroom and comes back with a white enamel basin of water and a yellow wash cloth. Sitting on the side of my bed, she spends the rest of the night bathing me with cold water to bring my fever down. She holds a glass of cool water for me to sip through a paper straw, but my throat is so sore, I can't swallow.

Doc Reckling is called to the house early the next morning. He tells me to open my mouth wide. He presses my tongue down with a flat piece of wood.

"Say, ahh," he instructs. He removes the little wood thingy and sticks a cold glass thermometer into my mouth. "Hold this under your tongue. Don't bite down on it."

The tiny glass rod feels funny. I worry it around with my tongue and try to keep it in place. The doctor removes the thermometer and peers at it through his half glasses.

"It's 103 degrees. Tonsillitis," he says. "We'll have to take those out once the swelling goes down and her temperature is normal."

The next morning the portly young doctor with the bushy moustache strides into our house trailed by a blast of fresh winter air. He brushes fluffy snowflakes off his black overcoat before removing and tossing it over the green upholstered chair where Daddy sits to read the newspaper. While he is taking my temperature, he notices the rough red rash on my chest.

"Looks like we have another case of Scarlet Fever," he tells Mother. "Your nephew, Jim has had a fever and rash for the past week." He retrieves a small white envelope from the pocket of his overcoat. "Here's a ten-day round of sulfa pills. Give her one every four hours. Make sure she drinks plenty of water. Keep her in bed and away from the other kids."

Before the doctor leaves, he carries me from my upstairs bedroom and helps Mother put me to bed in the little room off the kitchen where Jay normally sleeps. Jay and two-year-old Gwen will sleep upstairs with Marj. Within a couple of days both Jay and Gwen are crying with sore throats and high fevers. They are moved downstairs into the bedroom with me. Somehow Marj doesn't get sick.

A few nights later I'm awakened by the clamor of the wind rattling the windows and my mother calling out in panic, "Fred, Fred, call Doc Reckling."

Daddy comes through the door in his underwear. I've never seen my father without all his clothes on.

"What is it?"

"Gwen's temperature is 105. She's shaking all over."

"My God." He runs to the telephone. "Betty," he says to the switchboard operator, "it's an emergency. Get Doc Reckling on the line."

When Doc bursts into our house, he's wearing no coat. His night shirt is tucked into his trousers with the black suspenders pulled onto his shoulders. The front of his pants is not zipped. Not even buttoned.

"Weather's a real bastard tonight." He takes Gwen from Mother and bundles her in a wool blanket. "Convulsions. I need to get her to the hospital, into an oxygen tent and on fluids. An ice bath will probably help bring her temperature down," he mumbles to himself as carries her out into the storm.

Night after night, Mother sits at our bedside and bathes Jay and me. Her hair hangs limp. Her beautiful face looks like a white mask with big dark circles for eyes. I wake up one night to see her crying. I have never seen my mother cry. She tells me when I'm sad or hurt that big girls don't cry.

"I can't go on like this." She sobs into Daddy's shoulder.

He holds her tight and rocks back and forth.

"Will it never end?" she cries.

"Wish I could help you more, but I can't risk being away from work in this weather and have one of those damned pump jacks freeze up. Conoco tells us one less oil well producing puts the war effort in jeopardy."

"I know," she says. "If only Julia hadn't had to go back to Wounded Knee to help with her sick grandkids. She'd at least be here to cook and help during the day."

"Maybe your mother could come home early," Daddy says.

*****

Grandma had gone to California to visit my great-grandparents and Uncle Bruce at camp with the Army Air Corps. When Mother calls, she cuts short her month-long trip and rides the bus for two days and nights to come home.

Early the next morning I am so excited when Grandma rushes into our living room and drapes her coat and hat over the back of the couch where I now spend my days. "The bus from Cheyenne was so crowded with troops heading to Fort Robinson, I had to sit on my suitcase in the aisle. That last one hundred thirty miles about did me in."

"I'm sorry. I wouldn't have called if things weren't in such a mess," says Mother.

Two days later when Gwen is released from the hospital, Daddy takes her to Grandma's house where she stays for more than a month. Doc Reckling says for her to get well she needs to be away from the ruckus Jay and I create. I think he's trying to give Mother a rest.

Each evening after supper Mother and Daddy go to Grandma's house to play with Gwen. Marj stays with Jay and me. We don't get to see our baby sister until she is well enough to come home. I talk to her on the phone sometimes, but still miss her. I even miss her playing with my dolls and making a mess in my coloring book.

Jay won't stay in bed. He sneaks out and gets into trouble. His temperature is back to normal a couple of days after Grandma comes home. I am still running a fever, even after two rounds of medicine. Doc comes every day.

"Eva has rheumatic fever. She absolutely has to stay in bed until her temperature is normal or her heart could be damaged," he says. "She must not have any kids in to play. She needs to rest."

So each morning for the next four weeks, before he leaves for work at six, Daddy carries me from my bed to the living room couch. By the end of the first week, I'm so tired of spending each day alone on this couch. Coloring and playing with my paper dolls is no fun without my friend, Tina. My black cat, Sassafras, who prowls outside all night and into the wee hours of the morning, curls up beside me all day to sleep. He doesn't care about me.

To pass the time, I study the calendar on the wall with the picture of the five dark-haired little girls wearing dresses that are identical except for the colors—blue, pink, yellow, green and lavender. Daddy says they all have the same father and mother and were born in Canada on the same day. The quintuplets are four years older than I and are world famous. I try to imagine what it would be like to have so many sisters to play with.

During times when she is not busy, Mother teaches me to write the alphabet and my name. I learn to write my numbers to 100.

"You'll be ahead of the other first graders when you start school in the fall," she says.

I can hardly wait for the first day of school.

When Marj comes home from school each afternoon, I beg her to read to me.

"Oh, all right. What shall we read today?"

"Little Women." I feel sorry for little Beth, who is sick like me, but like Jo the best.

"I'll be glad when you learn to read for yourself." Marj moves my fuzzy black cat aside and plops onto the couch.

Later as I doze in a feverish trance, I hear the constant tap-tapping of the keys and the carriage return bell as Marj types articles for the Lusk High School newspaper on Mother's black typewriter with the word, *Underwood,* in gold letters on the front.

On Sunday mornings, following my breakfast of pancakes and maple syrup, Daddy helps me read the Denver Post colored Sunday funnies—"Little Orphan Annie", "Mutt and Jeff" and "Blondie".

Finally, when my temperature reads normal for two days, I'm allowed out of bed. After Mother helps me dress, she says, "Hold out your hand."

Into my hand she places a piece of Double Bubble. The fruity scent makes my mouth water.

"Mr. Dorf saved it back last week and sent it home for you."

"I'll give it to Jim. You know, that day at the store, he didn't get any so I let him chew mine a little while."

"Oh, Eva." She rests her head on mine. The dampness of her tears is warm on my skin. I don't know if she is happy or sad.

*****

Evelyn Neil, an award-winning author, began writing following retirement from a career as a small business owner/accountant. Her short stories appear regularly in anthologies and journals. Her memoir, DANCING TO THE END OF OUR RAINBOW, an indelible tale of love, despair and discovery explores end-of-life choices and is available on Amazon.com. Learn more on www.rmkpublications.com/evelyn-neil

Honorable Mention   **Jennifer Trotter**

Ghost on the Lawn

My sister and I were in the backyard catching fireflies in the early evening. The sky had grown dark.

From the house, a faint shaft of light, diffused by red checkered curtains wafting from the slightly open window, cast an eerie blood-tinted image that danced upon the grass. Jimmy Dean's "Big Bad John" blared from the kitchen radio:

> *Somebody said he came from New Orleans*
> *Where he got in a fight over a Cajun Queen*
> *And a crashin' blow from a huge right hand*
> *Sent a Louisiana fellow to the promised land, big John*

From that small window above our kitchen sink, my mother would be watching us while she washed our dinner dishes, making sure we were safe alone in our backyard at this hour, or so I thought.

The only other illumination came from the soft green-tinted flashes of light from the little bugs imprisoned in my glass jelly jar.

"Why don't you girls go catch some fireflies," mom had said right after we finished our meatloaf and mashed potatoes, handing us each empty jars with metal tops punched with breathing holes. "Your dad needs some peace and quiet."

"I'm not scared of the dark," said my sister, two years older than me and making me wonder if I should be afraid. She grabbed a jar and headed for the backyard. Like always, I followed her lead.

"I'll be right here watching from the window," Mom reassured us from the backdoor.

An above-the-sink window overlooking the backyard was a feature of every house in my neighborhood, all built in the 1950s from nearly identical floorplans.

At first I stayed near my sister. She was great at catching fireflies. She used both her hands to catch one, then moved it to one hand while she unscrewed the top of the jar with the other. When she saw me struggling to catch even one, she gave me a few of hers for my empty jar. Then I watched her run to the darkest part of the yard where she darted in and out of the tall bushes shrouded in shadows. She knew the greenery attracted the flickering bugs and that they were easier to see among the dark leaves. I didn't know that helpful little hint back then, when I was not yet six years old. Besides, the dark bushes frightened me. I imagined all sorts of monsters and creatures lurking there. I preferred staying out in the open.

I listened to the lyrics of the song floating out of the window:

> *Then a miner yelled out "there's a light up above!"*
> *And twenty men scrambled from a would-be grave*
> *Now there's only one left down there to save, big John*

I waited patiently where I stood thinking about big John, a murderer, who saved the lives of so many miners trapped in the dark. Then, I spotted a lone twinkle. I ran circles around the miniscule creature until it swooped down nearer the grass. I fell to my knees and, making sure I didn't squish it dead, carefully maneuvered it into the mouth of my slightly opened jar, taking care my few other captives didn't escape.

On the opposite side of the backyard, far from my sister and the shadowy bushes, another faint light blinked near the gate of the chain-link fence that opened to the front of our house.

Though I'd been warned often enough not to do so, I loved swinging on that gate, my feet balanced on the lower support pole so I could lean back and just skim the top blades of the grass, my hands clutching the upper pole.

I was thinking of doing just that, since I knew the gate would be out of my mom's watchful view from the window, when I heard a car approach, its headlight beams reflecting off our freshly paved street. I slowly opened the gate, cradling my jar in the crook of my arm. I knew

I was meant to stay in the backyard but wondered why the car was slowing down. I couldn't help but peek around the corner to see where it was heading.

It stopped in the street right in front of our house. The passenger-side door opened.

That's when I saw the ghost, all white flowing fabric, with black spots for eyes and a pointed head. It seemed to float ever so slightly above the lawn my dad had just mowed the day before, drifting toward our front door.

I stifled a scream and dropped my jar, glass shattering and fireflies escaping back into the shadows of the night. I turned and ran, terrified, into the backyard and then into the safety of my house through the backdoor.

My sister followed close behind me, asking what had happened...was I stung by a bee or something.

"I saw a ghost, I saw a ghost," I cried, nearly breathless, searching through the house for my mom and dad, tears of fright streaming down my cheeks.

"Nonsense," my mom rushed to envelop me.

Once my sobs subsided, I noticed my dad emerging from the hallway that led to the bedrooms.

"What did you really see?" He asked. My gaze fixed on the front door.

He walked through the living room to the picture window, the place where, each Christmas, we displayed our shiny silver aluminum tree with its bright pink ornaments. He pushed aside the curtain to look out front.

"Whatever you saw, there's nothing out there now. Come here, take a look yourself."

With a finger in my mouth, I slowly stepped to the window.

"Go ahead, don't be a scaredy cat. Take a look."

Cautiously, I peered out the window. The car and the ghost were nowhere to be seen.

"But there was a car, I saw it...," I insisted, "...and the ghost came out of the car and went right up to our front door."

"Time for bed," mom said. She looked tired.

In the middle of the night, the distant sound of a siren woke me for a moment, but sleep quickly overcame me again. Still, the ghost haunted my dreams—that night and many others to follow.

At breakfast the next morning, I heard my parents talking in low voices about a house, one only partially built several blocks away, that caught fire during the night.

"What happened?" My sister asked, never shy about finding out what was behind the whispers and secrets of any grownup.

"Nothing, really. There was a fire. The firetrucks came and put it out. No one lived there yet. No one was hurt," Mom said as she cleared our oatmeal bowls from the kitchen table.

Only later, much later, did I surmise that we lived then in an affordable house in a new suburb, a planned community where only White families were welcome.

Back in the early 1960s, when I was nearly six, I didn't know that fireflies tended to assemble in the coolness of the darkest shrubbery, or that hanging on a swinging gate could break it or perhaps hurt me, or that the postwar baby boom resulted in a profusion of new houses being built in newly developed subdivisions outside city centers, or that men like big John might be both good and bad, or anything about so-called "current events"—the growing antiwar movement, racial unrest, social injustice, and cultural prejudices.

Now, with the recent Black Lives Matter movement, I recalled that time in my childhood and pieced together what I likely saw that night long ago and the significance of that incident at that particular place and time in my life.

It was a sad, eureka sort of moment for me.

We lived at that time outside Evansville, Indiana. A place with a long history (I learned only recently) of Ku Klux Klan activity. The Indiana Klan, founded in Evansville in 1920 and boasting as many as 250,000 members in its earlier years, promoted ideas of racial superiority. Even today, it is purported to be the largest and most powerful branch of the northern Klan. While the Klan's influence faded over the years, in the 1960s, some attempted to revive it in response to current events like the Vietnam War, urban riots, and economic influences.

My family often drove past the burnt remains of that partially built house on our way in and out of our neighborhood. I never discovered if that fire was just accidental, a coincidence that it caught fire the same night I saw what I believed to be a ghost. What I now suspect is that the new construction in our all-White subdivision was likely meant to house a Black family.

I never talked about that night with my parents again. We soon moved away from that place, my mom had a baby (another girl), and then they divorced, resulting in my mom and us kids moving again, this time without my dad, to her hometown in the South.

My mom and dad, as well as my older sister, are all now deceased. I never discovered, but it would not surprise me today, if my dad actually was that ghost I saw long ago, a Klan member dressed all in white that night. I believe he might have admired and embraced the Indiana Klan chapter's claim of being a Christian fraternal organization promoting morality. I hadn't seen him leave the house after dinner, but then my sister and I were preoccupied, sent to the backyard by my mom to capture fireflies.

My grandparents and multiple previous generations are deeply rooted in central Louisiana, tracing their ancestry back to the earliest settlers of that southern state. Most of these families I knew only as poor farmers, blue-collar workers, or country tradesmen. Good, hard-working, community-minded people who struggled to earn a living, especially during the time of the Depression. Then I learned through genealogy research and census records that some on the branches of my family tree, back before the Civil War, owned tracts of fertile Louisiana farm land and some slaves—nameless people in those records I had found. My relatives weren't large plantation owners, still, discovering this saddened me and made me want to extend heartfelt apologies to the descendants of these nameless individuals on behalf of my ancestors. I would like to say to them *Sawubona*, a Zulu tribe word, a greeting, meaning "I see you" and you are important to me, I recognize your worth and dignity."

Growing up, I listened to my relatives, neighbors, and their friends, as well as my own parents and grandparents, openly express their prejudices in the privacy of their homes. I accepted their seeming anger and obvious disgust at, and general distrust of, all Blacks as something normal in my community, even if I didn't understand it. I increasingly began seeing Black children in the public schools I attended, though we seldom shared tables at lunch or space in the playground. Lessons learned in school and through social commentary blaring from the television seemed often contradictory to the conversations I heard at home. When I saw images of the Klan on the television nightly news, I didn't make the connection to what I saw on that night until much later in my life, the ghost who was actually just a man, likely my own father, wearing a bedsheet to hide his identity while undertaking some nefarious activity.

As years passed and, as all children do, I gradually gained knowledge about the world around me. I learned to separate what I thought and felt from my parents' and grandparents' core ideals. I considered abstract notions like fairness and equality and somehow came to reject many of their biases, to even challenge my mom directly about what she believed when it came to other races and cultures.

My mom made sacrifices to raise three daughters on her own. I wasn't always as grateful as I should have been, especially as a teenager. We disagreed about many things—clothes, hairstyles, curfews, and music, especially music. I embraced the pop culture and counterculture of my time opposing war and racism. I listened to songs like Bob Dylan's "Blowin' in the Wind" and "Abraham, Martin, and John" by Dion. I enjoyed blues, jazz, and rock and roll. My mother listened to country and western tunes. She hated my music; I hated hers (though I now find I enjoy bluegrass and traditional folk songs, even Dean's "Big Bad John," in spite of my earlier prejudices against my mother's taste in music). She even confessed to me once to liking Charlie Pride's songs, though she couched that admission saying something like, "he really doesn't sound like a Negro at all."

Though curious and a bit rebellious throughout my life, I only now better understand the ingrained barriers I had to cross, the misinformation I had to crush, and, ultimately, the beliefs I needed to reject—my parents' deep-seated beliefs—to create and develop my own view of the world. If I can recognize my own family and past generations for what they were and reject their racist ideals, others can as well.

I've come to accept, even embrace, my heredity. Afterall, we can't chose our ancestors. And, as I did when I was a child, I continue to seek any small bright light I can find in the world to lead me, even when it takes me into dark places, while learning to let go of those scary ghosts I witnessed throughout my life.

*****

With a Master's Degree in English, **Jennifer Trotter** (pen name Lynn Andrepont) is a former editor, journalist, researcher, marketer, teacher, and librarian spending time now perfecting her writing craft, dangling from her family tree searching for hidden branches, and exploring ancient ruins and remnants of lost societies.

See also https://www.southwestwriters.com/author-pages/author-pages-n-z/jennifer-trotter/.

Honorable Mention   **Joe Capello**

Once Upon a Midnight

I learned of my cousin Russell's passing on a Sunday morning. I remember holding the phone to my ear and looking out my front window as my brother delivered the bad news. The desert landscape in front of my New Mexico home resembled something out of a painting. The beauty and serenity of it contrasted with the bad news I now heard. As I hung up, memories of my 82-year-old cousin's younger days boiled to the surface.

Russell. My big cousin. A "cool" kid with the perfect 50's hair style, black, slicked back on the sides with a shock of it hanging over the middle of his forehead. The proud owner of a sleek Chevy Impala, black, red interior with posi-traction rear, as he was fond of saying. He loved that car. I can still see him washing it meticulously in the backyard of our house in East Orange, New Jersey.

"The secret," he used to tell me, "is to keep it wet until you're ready to dry it."

My "cool" cousin who defined the consummate "in" crowd of the 1950's. He could have been the twelfth man in the "Oceans 11" movie or a Fonzi equivalent, a good guy everybody looked up to, but also someone who knew how to handle himself. I once saw him face down two thugs at a parade we all attended at the Jersey shore. They were rough, burly guys dressed in faded dungarees and black leather jackets, hoods I thought could crush my skinny cousin with their bare hands. But he stood his ground and made them back down. I couldn't hear what he said to them, but I remember the look of fear in their eyes as they walked away from him.

But my fondest memory of my cousin Russ is the night he appeared on "The Alan Freed Show" in New York City.

*****

I was 12 years old in 1959 and any kid who ever listened to a radio or heard a rock 'n roll song knew Alan Freed. He was the host of "The Big Beat" show on Saturday's on WNEW TV in New York. Before Dick Clark and American Bandstand, there was Alan Freed. If you wanted to see all the hot singers and groups of the time, you tuned him in so you could show off your rock'n roll knowledge at school on Monday mornings.

Russ had answered an ad for pop singers he got from his mom, my Aunt Angie, a few months before. He went to a meeting with two guys from Charm Records. Before they even heard the demo recording he brought with him, they told him he had what it took to make it big. He could be the next teen idol like Frankie Avalon, Fabian or Bobby Rydell. They told him he had "the look."

Russ left the meeting with a contract in his hand to make a two sided record for Charm as well as the stage name "Russ Aladdin." After the record was released, Russ' manager got a call from Alan Freed offering him a guest appearance on an upcoming Saturday show.

*****

I could hardly sleep as I waited and even prayed for the Saturday night of Russ' scheduled appearance to arrive. It finally came and things started to move quickly. After dinner my father, mother, brothers and I went into the living room. Dad turned on our black and white Emerson TV adjusting it to eliminate the horizontal black waves that frequently rolled up and down the length of the picture tube and turning the brightness and contrast knobs to get as clear a picture as possible. He fiddled with the ears of the antenna, turning each one up and down until he found the position that gave the best reception.

We sat patiently waiting for the show to start. I remember recalling how adults at the time often ridiculed rock 'n roll music, lamenting the good old days of big bands and singers who were clean cut and "didn't shake all around when they performed."

But for me, rock n' roll was everything. It was free and brash, irreverent and fun. It could fill in the words for things we kids wanted to say but didn't know how. Jerry Lee Lewis singing, "Great Balls of

Fire" with the lyric, "You shake my nerves and you rattle my brains," were "way out" compared to Pat Boone's sappy "Love Letters in the Sand." The thought of my cousin joining the list of free wheeling rockers I idolized reverberated in my head as I sat with my eyes glued to the TV.

The show started and we all got quiet. Alan Freed looked into the camera and started talking in that scratchy, nasally voice of his that sounded like sandpaper on rock. His words echoed throughout the room.

"Man, you cats are gonna really love this bright new star I'm about to introduce. Here he is, someone you're gonna' hear a lot about, singing his new hit, 'Once Upon a Midnight,' Russ Aladdin."

The kids in the TV audience cheered. We all jumped up and down as the camera faded out, then hushed each other as it faded up on Russ. The intro bars to his record began to play. Russ looked into the camera and started lip syncing the words to the song.

"Once upon a midnight, in a land so very far, two lovers met on a hilltop, and wished upon a star." We were all on our feet crowding around the set, trying to edge in as close as we could to get the best view the 10 inch round picture tube could offer.

Russ continued. "Two young hearts that wished to be, forever and eternally, as one."

He looked into the camera. You could see in his eyes that he was someone who identified with the young lovers who wanted to be together forever. I had heard the song many times before, but this was the first time I realized he was singing to all the teenagers in America who were in love.

The song ended and the studio audience erupted in thunderous applause. We shouted and hooted in my living room. No doubt about it. My cousin was on his way to becoming a big star.

*****

I went to school the following Monday. A girl I had secretly admired for most of my grammar school years quietly came up to me.

"Was that your cousin on Alan Freed Saturday night?" I nodded. She smiled. "He was cool." Other kids shared their excitement with me about cousin Russ and how he would soon be a household name.

But fate intervened. After his appearance, record shop orders for Russ' record boomed. But Charm Records went bankrupt and couldn't press enough vinyl disks to meet the demand.

Alan Freed became embroiled in a payola scandal involving accepting payments from record companies to give their records airtime. In 1962, Freed was convicted on multiple counts of violating the new payola law. He never recovered from the negative publicity.

Russ went on to record a couple of more records and even made an appearance in 1960 on the then popular "Clay Cole Show" broadcast from Palisades Park, New Jersey. He sang two new songs, "Little Miss America," and "Annie Adorable." Although these recordings showed a lot of promise, nothing came of them.

At the time I often thought about how great it would have been if one of Russ' song made it to number one on the Billboard charts or if he appeared on the cover of some teen magazine like Bobby Darin or Frankie Avalon. I could have pointed him out and told all my friends, "That's my cousin." It wasn't meant to be. Still, there was a coda to the Russ Aladdin story that I wouldn't discover for several years to come.

*****

It was during a visit I made to cousin Russ a few years ago. After his music career ended, he became an insurance adjuster and enjoyed a successful career with a major insurance company before retiring to Florida.

We talked about the "Russ Aladdin" days. During our conversations, I learned how close he had come to joining the list of successful teen rockers at the time.

The exposure he received attracted the attention of a major music producer. This producer had the golden touch, and artists he represented at the time all went on to enjoy successful singing careers. He offered to sign Russ, a slam dunk if there ever was one.

But Russ decided to pass, putting his faith in his current manager and song writer. That one decision proved fateful; his career soon ended after that.

I couldn't help asking Russ if he regretted his decision. He came so close; it had to be a bitter pill to swallow. I still hear the answer he gave without hesitation.

"Not at all," he said. "I would have never had my kids if things went that way."

*****

These past few days I catch myself singing the words of Russ' song, "Once Upon a Midnight," over and over in my head. That is how most fairy tales I remembered as a kid began. And, like most fairy tales, they usually ended happily. Until now, I thought that happy ending eluded Russ. But after hearing the news of his death, I realized I was wrong.

He chose loyalty to friends and, ultimately, family over fame, and never looked back.

Not a bad ending for a fairy tale.

*****

Joe Cappello is most proud of two successes in 2022*: Sell Bots*, his one act play about workplace harassment, published in the Winter 2022 issue of **The Good Life Review**, and *The Secret of the Smiling Rock Man*, his short story, which won first place in the National Federation of Press Women's 2022 Communication contest.

Books by SouthWest Writers

*NOTE: Every book written by the SWW membership has received one or more national and/or regional awards.

Available on Amazon and at local Albuquerque bookstores

Ramblings and Reflections 2021 Annual Writing Contest Anthhology of Short Stories and Poetry.

Seeing the World in 2020 is the title of the Writing Contest anthology born during the first year of covid lockdown. It gave entrants an opportunity to express themselves at a time we were unable to participate in populated gatherings.

The ***2019 Annual Writing Contest Anthology of Short Stories and Poetry***. This was the year that began it all as SouthWest Writers initiated the writing contest as a tool to educate authors as well as showcase their quality.

The *Sage Anthology*, a collection of short stories, poetry and articles about writing by writers first published in the *SouthWest Sage* newsletter.

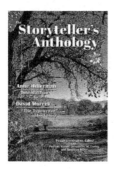

The *Storyteller's Anthology* was the first collection of stories by SWW members including Anne Hillerman, and David Morrell

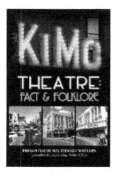

Kimo Theatre: Fact & Fiction. The KiMo Theatre is an iconic structure in Albuquerque, New Mexico that was built in 1927 to be a silent movie palace. SWW Members combined their skills to produce a book full of first person stories, historical data and photographs. The unique Pueblo Deco architecture combined with its history of theatrical and film events make it stand out as a historically fascinating place that is still in use today.

For more interesting writing and information access the SWW SAGE Newsletter through the website!

https://www.southwestwriters.com/sww-publications/newsletter

SouthWest Writers is a non-profit organization devoted to helping both published and unpublished writers improve their craft and further their careers. With over 450 members, SWW serves authors worldwide in every fiction and non-fiction genre through both in-person and virtual meetings, classes, workshops and by providing writing opportunities.

SWW has a database of professionals who offer services to potential authors including editing, web design, mentoring, formatting, illustrations, cover art, blogging, and information about self-publishing. For more information go to:

www.southwestwriters.com

Made in the USA
Las Vegas, NV
04 October 2022